Essay Index

SELECTED ESSAYS

SELECTED ESSAYS

OSCAR W. FIRKINS

KENNIKAT PRESS/PORT WASHINGTON, N. Y.

EDITOR'S NOTE

Grateful acknowledgment of permission to reprint essays included in this volume is hereby made to the *Atlantic Monthly* (Poetry Insurgent and Resurgent), *Modern Language Notes* (Has Emerson a Future?), *North American Review* (The Irresponsible Power of Realism, The Source of Pleasure in Familiar Plays, *and* What Happened to Hamlet?), *Poet Lore* (Poetry and Prose in Life and Art), *Saturday Review of Literature* (The Last of the Mountaineers), *Sewanee Review* (The Character of Macbeth), *Theatre Arts Monthly* (Action in Drama), and the *Yale Review* (The Ethics of Taste *and* Undepicted America).

CONTENTS

 SELECTED ESSAYS

MAN : A CHARACTER SKETCH

⊰⊱⊰⊱⊰⊱⊰⊱⊰⊱⊰⊱⊰⊱⊱⊰⊰⊰⊱⊱⊰⊰⊰⊱⊱⊰⊰⊰⊱⊱⊰⊰⊰

It is said that Herbert Spencer and Thomas Henry Huxley watched one day some young English swimmers by the seacoast; and they agreed that it was strange that Evolution should have chosen the animal type represented by those smooth, white young bodies for its standard bearer. Their points I loosely summarize from memory. They pitied the animal man for his weak hand with its flat, ineffectual nails, so different from the leopard's claws and the hawk's talons. They pitied him again for his mouth, a puny mouth, fit for nothing but to grind corn and shred meat, insignificant beside the power to seize and hold in a dog's muzzle. These are attractive speculations. They lead us to ask on our own account: Why was man the choice of Evolution?

The other, the rival, species in man's apish days would have foreseen his coming mastery as little as the boys who dived in the same swimming pool with the ten-year-old Herbert Hoover guessed that those little legs, no rounder and no nimbler than their own, would carry their owner to the White House. Why didn't the elephant build the first house? Its tusks would have been so useful in felling timber. Why didn't the giraffe paint the Sistine Chapel? Its neck would have been so serviceable for the ceiling. What would the falcon, the reindeer, and the horse have said if they had known that a meddling saucebox with a peering, jeering face would one day hold their lives in the bore of his rifle and their freedom in the twisting of his noose?

I have a notion of my own about this animal and his unexampled rise to power and mastery. I might say that, being a monkey, or at least an ape, he was a born climber, and that civilization was for him only another and a taller tree. But I prefer an idea that is not a figure. I suggest that man went so far for the simple reason that man could not sleep during all the hours he did not give to the seeking or the taking in of food. He woke up too soon; woke up before it was time for another meal or another hunt. He had a restless mind, a mortal fear of boredom, and nothing—for the moment—to do; so he civilized himself to kill time. While the cow was munching her turnips, and the pig was dozing in the sun, and the cat was tidying her fur, and the dog was scratching his fleas, man stopped a hole in the thatch of his nest, or strewed mosses instead of dried leaves on his bed. If he was bareheaded, he made himself a cap; if he had a cap already, he made a tassel for the cap. If his hut was dark, he made a window to let the light in; if he already had a window, he made a shade to keep the light out. He did this to comfort his body; but he did it quite as much perhaps to occupy his mind. This mind of his was a restless, fussy, prying, peeping, poking, tasting, nibbling, nuzzling, nipping, clipping, chipping, tampering, tinkering mind. The slang verb, "to monkey," exactly paints his disposition.

Here we have his starting point, not his best or greatest side, but his vital, fruitful, characteristic property. A bustling fellow, with his nose and finger everywhere, he stumbled one day upon heroism, he ran into genius. His curiosity was ravenous. "It's human natur' to be curus," said Hosea Biglow's Aunt Keziah. The apostle Paul and the orator Demosthenes both made exactly the same criticism of the Athenian people — they were always after some new thing. He was a wanderer, a seeker of new places. He hunted or, nomadic, tended flocks. One day he planted a seed in a slit in the earth. In that little act he planted much more than the seed; he planted himself. His very curiosity, hitherto urging migration, now bound him to the spot; he had to stay and see what would come up. He put himself eagerly into that long furrow, not guessing that the furrow was a rut. Then he made a house and a barn, and his babies lolled across the doorstep, and his chickens pecked the corn that dropped from the overrunning eaves. He was caught, he had to stay: but the roaming impulse still lingers in his blood. He makes all manner of things, but, more than anything else, he makes vehicles. Every farmer owns a wagon; every happy farmer (if there be such a thing) owns a car. He roams the world, but he now comes back. On Broadway he yearns for the desert and the jungle; in the desert and the jungle he pines for Broadway. He wakes in Africa from a dream of his wife and child in Baltimore to scare off the lion who has crept too close to his tardily replenished fire. He will run off from his warm settle by the hearth to that terrible sea that Masefield or that Conrad paints, and he will cross that sea to die on a hilltop or rot in a mudhole, singing "Over There."

Curiosity makes him a traveler: the same curiosity makes him avid of entertainment. He loves amusement, but, strangely enough, he is not very amusable. At a picnic he rarely looks cheerful; at a film he is little less than moody. He will tell you that he is very fond of stage plays, but most of the very few plays that managers dare to offer to him are frozen off the stage by the iciness of his demeanor. He invented the fine arts for his enlivenment, and in Florence the American wife can hardly drag the husband into the Uffizi. If he goes to church once a week, he hires high-priced vocalists and high-priced orators to prevent an hour with God from becoming unbearably tedious, and even then the part he most enjoys is the benediction.

The truth is that few amusements hold him beyond those in which he actively participates. I except football; I except pugilism: but, in general, this restless and nimble being abhors passivity. His fun is action, because he wants to feel, not other people, but himself. He sleeps in church; he nods in the theater. In a Six o'Clock Club, where the members are mostly passive, the most popular item in the constitution is the by-law which closes the meeting at eight o'clock sharp. Reading is too passive. Enormous as the outgush of print is, man is not inherently a reading animal. Few men can read anything but newspapers; few women can read anything but novels. Man has indeed small comfort either in the page or pen; he is too active to read, and he is too lazy to write. The action that he craves must be voluntary. His play, if his soul forsakes it, becomes work; his work, if his soul passes into it, becomes play. Moreover, he is so ingenious that the things he can make or do are more exciting than the things he can imagine. With an airplane whirring over his head, what interest has the Arabian's imagined flying horse for him? He spawns monsters in his own workshop. What should he do with Greek mythology?

Like many other parts of man, his self-love is always restless and experimental. One day long ago, after many trials, the man-ape discovered the secret of breaking a cocoanut without spilling the milk. His next step was to tell his wife. Wifehood in those early days was placable, and she admired his dexterity. His heart melted, and he gave her all the milk to drink. This was a turning point in his career; he had made two discoveries, not one; and the second was, that admiration was delicious. He has never convalesced from this discovery. From this time on he planted, he nursed, he watered, he pruned, he fondled, his image in the minds of his household and his clan. No other creature is fantastic in this kind to this degree. To this image he will sacrifice the solidest, the most indispensable, realities. To feed this image he will go hungry. An American physician in the public eye went forty days without food. On a desert island he would have succumbed in forty hours. Even in his civilized state man will spend useless, wearing, and exasperating hours on cross-word puzzles with the aim of impressing somebody who hates him for his victory. An explorer will go to a fearful place at the apex of the world, where there is nothing to see and almost nothing to do, in order to be patted on the back on his return by some fellow who had brains enough to stick to his own chimney corner.

The truth is that man is half a mountebank, meaning by that word, not a rogue, but a performer. Half of his early primal sense consists of meddlingly curious inquiry; the other half consists of showmanship. These two traits have almost been the chisels of his destiny. Do you wish to know why he is so given to conversation, why, very possibly, he invented speech? Because in mutual speech his two great primary instincts, curiosity and showmanship, are both indulged. When he listens, he indulges the first; when he speaks, he indulges the second. Conversation is very happy in the treadle-like alternation of these stimuli. It is curious and astonishing to note how in our time the profoundest and gravest scientific study emerges into forms which appeal to one or both of these dominating instincts. Invention is multiplex, but what are its main lines, the lines, at least, that are foremost for the public? They are of two sorts: they help man to go faster and farther, or they help man's word to go faster and farther. The great mechanical expedients, wheel, railway, steamship, submarine, airplane, telegraph, telephone, wireless, radio—with what eagerness, so to speak, they speed to range themselves in one or other of these mighty categories! Yet travel in any form is a feeder to curiosity, and communication in any form is a means of self-display. Everything puts on the aspect of a show. An airplane is half a skyrocket; a Zeppelin is almost a trapeze. The popular name for the great scientific adept just lost to America is the wizard—that is to say, the showman. In his aërial solitude, between earth and sky, between life and death, the aviator dreams of headlines.

Man lives, as no other creature lives, in this reflected image of himself in other minds. In the country he feels it strongly; packed into cities, he feels it still more. Civilization, pressing men together in a straitened world, augments the chance for criticism, the itch for criticism, and the fear of criticism. The light in which he views almost everything is the light that is shed upon that thing by the eyes of his fellow men.

The view of man thus far expounded has been low—too low, as I willingly and thankfully concede. But these are foundations; it is now my task to relate them to the superstructure. Man is not only restlessly and contrivingly curious; he is not only a performer on a stage; he is plastic. His ingenuity and his plasticity work together in a felicitously complemental way: his ingenuity fashions new conditions, and his plasticity reshapes him in the mold of these conditions. As the conditions are various, the results of the plasticity are various; and man becomes almost at a logical bound the most diversified and versatile of living types. He embraces almost a whole zoology within a species.

Let us see how the two traits work together. The ingenuity of man, the nomad, builds a house; then his plasticity turns him into a house man. Still more does it turn the woman who stays in the house—I am referring to ancient times—into a house woman. The ingenuity of man, the landsman, builds a boat; he enters the boat, and his plasticity converts him into a marine animal. When he finds that results are better when one man does one thing than when every man does everything, he chains each man to one thing by a trick which he calls the division of labor, and this man is then melted down and recast in the mold of his specialty. Often, by doing one thing, he becomes a mere tool; then one of his too clever brethren invents an iron or a wooden tool that will do his work, and he is turned off, sad in heart, because he is a tool that wants a dinner.

He casts into new molds not merely his body and his habits, but his heart and spirit; he makes mental and moral experiments which, if successful, reconstruct their maker. Light creature as he is, half tinker, half mountebank, he can become serious and severe, he can become stern and savage. Through habit, under pressure, under stimulus, he will in chosen individuals explore and compass every possibility. With an apelike agility he (the race, not the individual) will speed from the bottom to the top, from the top to the bottom, of every intellectual and moral ladder; he will rise to heroism and genius, he will sink to depravity and imbecility. He will invent martyrdoms, he will hunt out filthiness, either of which, if unproved, would have been held to be impossible. It is part of his nature to coerce and to reverse his nature. The diameter of that nature is amazing. The most impressive of all conceivable tableaux to me is that of a harlot and a nun, each looking into the other's eyes, and each conscious that she might have been the other. The celibacy both of nuns and priests, the renunciation by thousands of persons, mostly undistinguished in mind, will, or character, of one of the most powerful and one of the most treasured of human appetites, ought to crash upon us like a thunderbolt. We are so used to the unimaginable in man that we scarcely lift our eyes to notice it.

The species, however, in all these ascents and descents keeps a certain hold upon itself. Look at industry, for instance. Look with Markham at the "Man with the Hoe," look with Hauptmann at the man by the loom, look with Zola at the man with the pick, and you will ascribe to the animal before you prodigious industry, heroic fortitude, and sublime patience.

True for the individuals, but not for the species. Even these prodigies will stop work if they can. A few rare toilers love their work. Edison may work till two A. M., but he will excuse his typewriter at five P. M. Typewriters will not work till two A. M.—not even for Edisons. For "typewriter" read "species." Idleness is the badge of gentility; it is more valued as a badge than as a privilege. The American pioneer, whose first name was Jabez, hardened his muscles into iron in the January blizzard; his son or grandson, whose first name is Sidney, turns his flesh into gruel in the steaming bathtub.

So much for labor and endurance; let us glance at courage. This quality, seemingly the hardest of human virtues, is among males the commonest. Thieves, liars, sots, and rakes are often courageous (recall *What Price Glory?*); yet what are the sacrifices required by truth, temperance, or honesty compared with those exacted by fearlessness in war? A man like you and me goes to a ridge in France; flight possible, every nerve imploring flight, amid bullets that make the readers of newspapers in distant clubrooms shudder, the extraordinary creature holds his ground. Strangest of all, the very woman from whom the next bullet may part him forever binds him to the spot. A whole tradition, a whole people, unite to send him there and keep him there. But the species, so to speak, looks on with an indulgently ironic smile. Months pass, and the marvel returns to his admiring country. But here he is no longer a marvel: his ear is agape for praise, his mouth for drink, his pocket for bonuses; at Detroit he will shout "I want beer," his poor throat clamorous about its own privations. His heroism in France was human only in the sense that it is human — very emphatically human — to do extraordinary things under extraordinary pressures.

The relation of these manifestations to the species begins to be clear. Heroism and treachery are not proper to the species; they are proper to individuals: what they evince in the race is merely its tendency to move in all directions in select individuals to the termini of all its possibilities. These various and contradictory developments prove just one thing about the species, its passion for exploration, for experiment, and for extremes. From the extremes it returns like a singer who, neither secure nor comfortable at the highest or the lowest note in his broad gamut, is glad to get back to the ease and sureness of his middle register.

At this point we are faced with a question. A species explores. Should not exploration lead to the discovery of kindlier regions, physical, mental, moral; lead, finally, to migration and settlement? This is the ideal outcome. In emigration, in mechanics, it is the real outcome. A motor, on land, or sea, in air, can be good enough to drive all other motors off the globe. With things moral and intellectual the case is different. An elementary virtue like honesty crops out everywhere, yet in thousands of years it cannot drive its abject rival, dishonesty, off the planet. Every village has its rogue. The race cannot be made a unanimous convert to its own good; and its own good is not always single, nor always clear. Hence vast range and great diversity in things mental and moral between the peoples and within the peoples of our sphere. Individuals, however, find in these new lands which the exploring race discovers but refuses to inhabit an abiding place which is their only key to the beauty and significance of life. The right of the single man to choose *against the race* is indefeasible.

From this diversity in men flow interesting consequences. Man is the great lawbreaker; that somewhat masks the fact that he is also the great lawmaker. You are amazed at his insubordination; I am amazed at his passion, almost his mania, for knotting himself up in a coil of laws, regulations, standards, ideals. Go to a law library: do not sit and read; simply stand and look; shelf upon shelf, wall upon wall, room upon room, level upon level, you have before you the vast printed record of the attempts of this creature to bind himself down and lock himself in. The vertical depth of a society is great: the estimable top makes laws for the disreputable bottom; the disreputable bottom amuses itself by breaking these laws, an amusement in which it is not infrequently joined by the estimable top. In relation to laws man seems to me exactly like a being who, in his love of fashion, buys a coat that is far too tight for him, and afterward, in his love of comfort, goes mostly in his shirt sleeves. Man, in this matter, is quite unfair to himself. How good and wise ought man to be at a given time and place? Is he bound to answer that question? Perhaps not. But he does answer it over and over again; he answers it in laws, regulations, standards. Then he shows by his own conduct how wise and good he really is; and the difference, which is his own work, is damning. I am not denying the necessity for some, at least, of these regulations; I merely say that man, in this matter, is unjust to himself; he is incriminated by his aspirations.

Those aspirations joined to his diversity and to the already noted willingness to sun himself in the eyes of his fellows are responsible for what I love least in his disposition. When he sees a great act or word, he wishes to perpetuate and disseminate that act or word. He forms an institution (for he can do nothing good without systematic reminders), and invites everybody to join. Sometimes everybody does join; the featherheads, the blockheads, and the time-servers join. The institution becomes hypocritical. An organization may be sincere, if it be low-pitched; it may be sincere if it be small; but if it is at once high in purpose and popular in reach, hollowness becomes inevitable.

If you wish to convince yourself that man is not a religious animal, go to church; if you want evidence that he is not patriotic, visit Congress; if you are hungry for proofs that he is indifferent to learning, join a university; if it would comfort you to believe that

he is bellicose, attend a peace conference. These conclusions would not be wholly just; it is far from unreservedly true that men are irreligious, unpatriotic,
indifferent to learning, and adverse to peace. But the
institutions are backsliders. Let me make my thought
precise. Man's *wish* to be better than his present self
is the best thing in him; man's *claim* to be better than
his present self is despicable: yet his whole society is
framed upon the assumption that the claim must precede and promote the fulfillment of the wish. Let us
look at two examples.

A congressman as congressman is selfish beyond the
high human average in that particular; yet he dare not
in public utter a single political sentiment that is not
disinterested. An American banker or lawyer or physician joins a church. He professes to adopt Jesus Christ
as his pattern. Now let us suppose that the difficulties
in this difficult undertaking are miraculously smoothed
away. Without exertion on his part, he is offered the
character of Jesus Christ on a silver platter, as it were,
to be his thenceforth in its fullness and entirety. *He
would not take that offer.* His reason for this is hu-
manly intelligible and forgivable: he does not wish
to become unrecognizable to his wife and children.
I do not condemn these institutions; they bend to a
necessity. But that necessity is the thing that I like least
in my kind. I wish I belonged to a species that was
good enough — or bad enough — to be candid about its
own nature. So far as I know, every other animal, from

the mastodon to the louse, plants itself firmly and contentedly upon its own being. Man alone departs from this content; he departs by a high path, aspiration; and again, by a low path, play-acting.

Many years ago the earlier Oliver Wendell Holmes, discriminating between three professions, remarked that the lawyers were the cleverest, the ministers the most learned, and the doctors the most sensible. The lawyers continue to be rather clever, the doctors to be fairly sensible; on the learning of the ministers let the laity preserve a seemly silence. My immediate subject, however, is man, and I wish to find out whether man's intelligence, of which there can be little question, takes the form of cleverness or sense. To my mind, he is clever rather than judicious. Tinker and mountebank, he excels in ingenuity. He has a cunning to make the gods (if gods there be) blush by comparison. What did Jupiter, what did Zeus, what did Odin, what did Jahweh, ever do that is comparable for sheer brain power to the invention of the sewing machine or spinning jenny? God let poor Noah build his own ark. God has so little to do. I think there is plausibility in that scene in *Green Pastures* — a play favored by the clergy — in which the Lord accepts a five-cent cigar from Noah. I am not a smoker myself, but the leisure of Omnipotence without a pipe is inconceivable.

Man's diversity takes him in all directions; necessarily, it takes him sometimes in the direction of common sense. Individuals often abound in the quality.

The pressure of need, present or past, has distributed the virtue through whole classes or layers of that broad Teutonic stock to which, by filiation or adhesion, most of us belong. Nevertheless, in spite of inventive America, industrial Germany, and commercial England, I doubt if sense be deeply rooted in that miraculous vertebrate that bears the name of man. His common sense, often strong within its fold or pen, instantly fails him when he forsakes the inclosure, whereas his cleverness is always on the watch for the appropriation of new territory. The tradesman whom in his hardware shop no swindler, no counterfeiter, no smug salesman, no specious mendicant, can make a fool of believes, in a political mass meeting, that Democrats or Republicans or even Progressives can distill prosperity from the ink on a statute book. The banker, undeceivable among bonds or borrowers, will follow a whisper or a wink from Wall Street into ruin. One of the main proofs of my contention is Wall Street itself, that wind-swung vane on the top of the economic structure, whose turnings, it is said, can make the whole solid edifice revolve.

Man lacks the larger common sense, the eye for aims and for proportions. The saying that common sense is rarer than genius is untrue, but the man who said it meant the truth that I am trying to express more cautiously. The pressing illustration of this defect in man is war. The case against war is equally overwhelming and simple; it would convince a philosopher or a child.

The spirit says "No," the reason says "No," and the poor little flesh, so often at abject odds with the reason and the spirit, cries out with a still louder voice "Amen." Yet man continues even after an eruption to replant his cot on the flank of Vesuvius. A brave nation would not shrink from what a brave Minneapolitan called the other day "disarmament by example." Yet men, who can stop war when they please, go on preparing for battle, and, if President Hoover meditates a pause in the building of warships, the Navy men, adepts naturally in the plumbing of abysses, declare that his ignorance is "abysmal."

England and America rank high among nations in political (not perhaps in diplomatic) sagacity, yet even here there is gas in the elector's brain. The last three presidents in our country have been chosen by majorities which in relation to their powers and services were fantastic. In Great Britain for the first time in its history the electorate is a virtual unit behind a government which is not itself a unit and whose platform is reducible to a single dubious plank; such unanimity is featherbrained. Is man saner in his economics? Insert into any of our high-class factories a single machine working as badly as the whole economic world-machine of which that factory is a part, and the passage of that machine to the junk heap would be an affair of days or hours rather than of twelvemonths. For this man is not altogether to blame, since the situation has closed down upon him like the lid of a trap. But let us ask one question. What percentage of the available intellect of the race, a race which has brains to spare for geology and archeology and anthropology and what not, is man applying to the solution of this vast and critically urgent problem? One per cent? Far less, I should suppose, than one per cent.

I confess to some leniency for those human vices which moralists have most persistently bewailed. Man is earthy, but the earth in his spirit, like the earth under his feet, seems to me rather part of his condition, his fortune, and his problem than his guilt. He is self-centered, but I do not find that unforgivable in the inhabitant of a planet that revolves round its own axis. His temper, the restless, meddling, posturing, plastic temper, does not seem to me to be primarily voluptuous. He is strongly sexed, of course, but, given the force of sex, I am much more struck by his restraint, for which he gets no praise from anybody, than by his undisputed outbreaks and excesses. That an animal should sometimes practice adultery does not astonish me so very much; what overwhelms me is that this same animal should have invented marriage. I grant that he is greedy, but even here he is more of a gamester and a performer than of a grubbing heaper-up of goods or coin. This is true particularly of those vast and futile fortunes which are amassed mainly for the fun of it and which are worn as ornaments or set up as trophies rather than applied to any solid — even to any solidly selfish — use.

The gorilla, man's kinsman, is ferocious, but man, when made comfortable, is good-natured: not seldom he is moderately kind. Primitive man's differentia from other species is rather intellectual than moral; as to good will or ill will, he is neutral or plastic. Give him leisure, safety, and a beam of sunshine, and he is impelled to be kind to somebody, even though to gain these benefits he has been cruel to somebody else. The unreclaimed man's attitude may be stated thus: If there is straw for only one, he will push his neighbor off that straw; but if there is straw for two, he will move aside to give his neighbor place. He will pat a dog with the hand with which he has just wiped a bayonet and he will soothe a child—even his neighbor's child—with the voice with which he has just cursed an enemy. Teach him love, teach him hatred, and he is an apt pupil. Hamilcar made his little son Hannibal swear on the altar undying enmity toward Rome. The boy swore, and kept his vow; but the point is that Hamilcar had to bind him by an oath; a hawk has no occasion to bind its fledglings to undying enmity with chickens. Man is almost invariably kind to the fruit of his loins, and he has been known to be content to lie by the same woman's side for fifty years. Once in a while, in one of his moral voyages, he loves his race, and in rare spirits, under rare incitements, the feeling puts on loveliness and grandeur.

Stevenson, in a noble essay called "Pulvis et Umbra," speaks of the rough man, "living mainly on strong drink, fed with affronts, a fool, a thief, a comrade of thieves, and even here keeping the point of honour and the touch of pity — still obscurely fighting the lost fight of virtue, still clinging, in the brothel or on the scaffold, to some rag of honour, the poor jewel of their souls!" The saving, final grace which Stevenson seeks in honor I would rather find in worship, worship not of the supernatural but of the higher forms of nature, an impulse which, to my mind, is the parent of all that is best in religion. A man, loving some quality in himself, sees that quality bettered in another man, and loves his fellow for its sake. He learns reverence and affection. I do not class this among the splendid exceptional manifestations which his exploring and experimental instinct brings to light; I value it as a property of the common man. The object, in the untaught man, may be low; but even then the passion, being disinterested, does not sink to the level of its object. Babe Ruth, Gene Tunney, John Gilbert, Al Capone — each has his court, his congregation, his Theban band; Milton admired his Miltonic devil. But the passion gains immeasurably in height and depth when it turns toward such objects as Bayard, Lincoln, Galileo, Jesus. There is a shrine for every divinity, and a worshiper for every shrine.

Sometimes with Anatole France I could "despise man tenderly"; sometimes I think I am fond of him — a little way off; sometimes I think I love him a little without liking him at all. When all is said, the word "human" is a kindly word. It does not acquit, but it convicts and pardons in a breath. Moreover, this cruiser man in his explorations of the planet has fallen half by chance upon a coast which I shall name the higher beauty and virtue. In his later voyages that may not be his goal; it may be only a port at which he touches. But at that port I, a passenger in his ship, if I be strong and wise enough, may disembark. And for that privilege my thankfulness to him shall be eternal.

SHELLEY AND OUR TIME

⇛⇛-⇛⇛-⇛⇛-⇛⇛-⇛⇛-⇛-⇛⇛)≪≪-≪-≪≪-≪≪-≪≪-≪≪-≪≪

Percy bysshe shelley died in 1822. The wind, the water, and the fire had each successively its share in the restoration of his mortal part to that Nature whose beauty had been echoed in his verse and mirrored, after all suspensions and abatements, in his conduct. Has this man who, dying at thirty, had seen the Congress of Vienna and its ghastly sequels, any comfort or message for us who have looked with doubting eyes at the issues of the Congress of Versailles? He is part, beyond question, of our imperishable memories; is he also by any chance part of those hopes which, in the recession of our dreams, we scarcely dare to call eternal?

Of all poets who loved images intensely Shelley is the poet most dominated by the passion for the universal. Other singers end with the universal; Shelley begins there. With Spenser it is form and color loved first as form and color and afterwards as message and abstraction; with Wordsworth it is linnet and celandine loved first as bird and flower and afterwards as spokesmen of the cosmos. Shelley begins at the whole. Sensuous, like all poets, he is; but he is sensuous to the total or the mass. His distinction might be conveyed in the remark that he loves the concrete without valuing the particular. Take the landscapes that brighten his work everywhere; what is mainly felt is the web, the network, the boscage, the embosomment; the whole is not the total of the units but the unit itself. Where other poets talk of lights and sounds and odors, the particulars, Shelley talks of light and sound and odor, the abstractions. If he fixes on a particular, it is the most evanescent or the most impalpable of objects, the invisible "West Wind," the melting "Cloud," or a "Skylark" reduced by distance to a song in the air. The heat of his imagination softens and half dissolves the landscapes. The philosophy which consorts with this temper, the philosophy, in a word, which unifies by dissolution, is pantheism; and the *Necessity of Atheism* is followed in a little more than five years by the "Hymn to Intellectual Beauty." Shelley is the poet who *blends;* in that he excels all other poets, as he falls below most other poets in the capacity to separate.

It is the same way with the characters. They are symbols or impersonations. Sometimes he calls his personifications the Earth and the Moon, sometimes Asia or Emily, sometimes Jane or Harriet or Mary. He loves men in their totality. If beyond most singers he is the poet of solitude, he is also beyond most the poet of that "multitude" which Mr. Masefield opposed to "solitude" in the title of a half-forgotten novel. What troops and companies in *Prometheus Unbound!* What throngs and aggregates in *The Revolt of Islam!* His very abstractions flock together in "solemn troops and sweet societies." His enthusiasm, as all readers know, is public — embraces the *res publica* in its strict etymological sense. The force — more especially the *initial* force — of this passion in Shelley is one of the signs and wonders of literary history. Visions of limitless benefit to mankind irradiated even his boyish experiments in chemistry and physics. At Eton he was already a mouthpiece of the revolutionary gospel. He was prepared at eighteen for Godwin's *Political Justice,* a book which handles the widest of aggregates, mankind, in relation to the highest of abstractions, happiness and justice. The empire of principles and aggregates over Shelley's mind is nowhere more evident than in the instant conquest which a book without beauty or imagery or passion made of a spirit for which beauty and imagery and passion were the inspiration and the goal of being.

From that time the apostleship was unbroken. Doubtless Shelley had other passions than the well-being of his kind, for after all man is man; but in its own field this disinterestedness was seemingly absolutely pure, uncontaminated with that love of domination, of publicity, of combat, which spot the purity, even while they feed the force, of the self-devoting impulses even in chosen minds. It is omnipresent in his work; even *The Cenci,* in which he comes closest to the attitude of the impartial dramatist or *trouvère,* is an illustration of resistance to tyranny in which the criminal is blent with the heroic. Everywhere he is the man commissioned and ordained, and his commission and ordination derives its sanction from nothing less august than the indwelling spirit of the universe and the everlasting interests of man.

There is a fact about this gospel which is hardly less remarkable than its nobility — its entire separation from tradition. Love of the race, though rare in its intenser forms, like all intensities, is neither new nor strange in European history, and the steps or routes to its attainment can be defined with reasonable precision. There is, first of all, Christianity, a religion which, with varying wisdom but unflagging perseverance, *does* impress upon its votaries a concern for the welfare of humanity. There is, secondly, that process, so easy in logic if so tedious in practice, by which a man's interests broaden outward from self to family, from family to nation, from nation to world. The strange thing about Shelley is that his benevolence drew aid or subsidy from neither of these sources. He seems the single ascertained instance of a powerful imagination that took no print whatever from the substance or the forms of the cult to which its childish sensibility was exposed. Shakespeare is a capital example of the extent to which an adherent of Christianity can de-Christianize his imagination; yet the microscope can discover even in Shakespeare allusions to men who have "been where bells have knoll'd to church." In Shelley the obliteration seems complete. He cannot even hear with Hauptmann the tolling of the "sunken bell" from the abyss.

His atheism, so called, seems a recoil, not from the national or local or parental cult, but from a speculative religion detected in a survey of the universe from an abstract pinnacle.

There remains the other approach, the steps of which are self, family, nation, world. In Shelley this graduation is destroyed by the virtual abolition of the second and third steps, and an argument for the absence even of the first might be urged in his behalf with less unreason than in the case of any other of the sons of men. But, avoiding the debatable, the boyish Shelley appears to have been strangely wanting in those family feelings to which by birth and nurture he was powerfully called. An early comradeship with sisters is more readily explained by their inclusion in a sex that he loved than by their place in a family to which after boyhood his indifference was palpable. Among all his landscapes there is scarcely one that appears to be riveted to a real place by the power of childish memories. A man so unattached to stock or soil would tend to be deficient in that national feeling to which race and place are such effectual contributors. To Shelley, England was a land to be specified between two others (Florence, Albion, Switzerland) in a list of the passers forward of the torch of freedom, or to be coupled with Spain in somewhat slighting comparison in a passage of the dithyrambic "Ode to Liberty." His satire, which would have been thought ruthless in a pamphleteer, was reserved almost or quite exclusively for his mother country. On this side, as on the sides of family and religion, the tradition had apparently nothing to do with the generation or the nourishment of his benevolence.

There is a third point about the Shelleyan passion for humanity that is akin to the second and is even more astonishing. We commonly expect that a passion which is *general* in its object and *disinterested* in its views will be derivative rather than original, will be less impulsive and less instinctive than passions of grosser quality and slighter scope. Shelley, living among the emotions that least conduce to spontaneity, was more spontaneous than the poets who restrict their verse to love and spring and wine. Matthew Arnold in a famous essay praises the divine liquidness of Chaucer's diction, the divine fluidity of his movement. With all deference to Chaucer, let us nerve ourselves to say that the liquidness, the fluidity, of Chaucer are comparable with Shelley's as the earthly is comparable with the divine. After Shelley it becomes a form of *lèse-majesté* to apply the words to other poets.

The spontaneity is inborn and indefeasible; it triumphs over all impediments; drama cannot halt, nor narrative retard, its fluency; through difficulties of meter, through involutions of syntax, the stanza moves with unchecked pliancy and grace. Will you have a quatrain that shall at once illustrate the spontaneity and describe the inauspicious themes with which it is so unbelievably combined?

I sang of the dancing stars,
I sang of the daedal earth,
And of Heaven — and the giant wars,
And Love and Death and Birth.

There is the cosmic theme of Emerson treated with more than the lyric unarrestedness of Burns. It is at this point that Shelley touches the absolute, justifies the hyperbole that affirms him to be poetry embodied. This does not imply that he is the greatest of poets; savor is often the product of admixture, and the quintessential is not always the supreme. But in Shelley, for good or ill, the feeling is pure not so much in a moral as in a chemical sense, and the verse is pure after the same fashion. In him, as in no other poet, a bound is reached, a process is completed, a type is embodied, a definition is framed; without reaching the absolute summit, he nevertheless answers the question "What is poetry?" better than Shakespeare, Sophocles, or Dante. By the conversion of pure passion into pure melody he achieves a poetry of which removal from earth is the dominating attribute, and all the time, by the strangest of miracles, he never flags in the enforcement of a gospel whose end is the renovation of the world.

In Shelley, then, the leading traits are three: the cult of humanity, the severance of that cult from tradition, and the association of that cult with faith and ardor. Our age is curiously like him in the first and second of these points; it is curiously unlike him in the third. In this combination of striking difference with striking similarity is the key to Shelley's relevance for our time.

Of course Shelley's renunciation of the past does not agree with ours in all particulars. The classical tradition, which loosens its hold on us, retained for him its full force, while the patriotism which he cast aside or never found abides with us in unreduced vitality. But, apart from patriotism, which is nothing more than a confined philanthropy, the sense of brotherhood is almost our only salvage from the wreck of the great ideals in which that sense once found its bulwark and its stay. We turn upon man the gaze we avert from God; our doubt of a soul makes us tender of the body; our lessened hope of a tomorrow imparts new values to today. The one thing which is quite clear to us in the dusk of our uncertainties is the actuality of human suffering, and the relief of whatever portion of that suffering is relievable is the object for which generous spirits everywhere are ready to unite. Poor and weak as we are, there are still men who will go to the trench or the grave in wartime for the welfare of a section of mankind, and there are also men who will go to prison in wartime for the sake of another view of the interest of mankind in its entirety. The partisans and the adversaries of Bolshevism assail each other with an energy which doubtless springs in many cases from an equally sincere concern for the welfare of their common charge — humanity.

The will to serve is righteous, even noble; its failing in our time is the divorce of charity from faith and hope, its aloofness from vision, warmth, and aspiration. The hand is ready but the heart is cold. The practice of beneficence is an industry, or a habit, or a mechanism, or an apology, or a decency, or a precaution; at its very best it helps man as one extracts a thorn from the foot of a crying dog, for whom a little more pain or a little less sums up the pitiful alternatives of an ungracious destiny. The dustiness of our philanthropy is sadly manifest in its emotional appeals, in which, however good the cause and sound the purpose, the *feeling* is obviously manufactured. Once beneficence leaned upon Christianity; the shrunken speech and widening industry of our churches would suggest that in our day Christianity leans upon beneficence; the priesthood passes into a diaconate.

Plainly, our need is a restoration of vision and fervor, and plainly again, the restorers will scarcely be found among men in whom the ideals that we retain depended for nourishment and support on ideals that we have forsaken. Even in search of a prophet we shall have a difficulty in recrossing the chasm that divides us from Moses, and Gregory the Great, and King Alfred, and St. Francis, and Las Casas, and Florence Nightingale, and Father Damien. Here lies our need of Shelley. The difficulty of preserving enthusiasm in the effacement of tradition finds its apt, perhaps its sole, physician in the man by whose unequaled force and fire that difficulty was triumphantly surmounted. Here is the example, decisive even if unique, that passions of the widest range and most impersonal quality may rival in intensity the demands of the senses, that a principle may be worshiped like a star, that a race may be loved like a woman. Shelley in a sense was shipwrecked like the rest of us, but the isle on which his keel grated before it split and sank was Patmos. Or, if a figure more congenial to our hurrying times be sought, it was a good moment in mechanics when men discovered that the electricity which propels the car could supply it from its own unaided powers with warmth and light. Our age has the motive force without the light, without the heat. Shelley is the invaluable and abiding proof that their separation need not be eternal.

THE SECRET TREASURE

In the social growth of man action and speech are the leaders; thought and feeling are the stragglers in the rear. Nature's chief business as an agent is to get things done; man's function as a social being is apparently to get things said. Nature in plants and minerals forges ahead briskly without aid from mind, and if, in the higher types and pre-eminently in man, she adopts feeling as a ram and thought as a compass, it is plain that what she wants is their help and not they. Man in his harness of consciousness is still uneasy like Crusoe's Friday in his European clothes. He is niggardly of thought and feeling; by the two admirably lazy shifts of reflex action and habit he shirks the greater part of psychic life. To speech he is much more favorably disposed; speech, like walking or chewing, is a muscular act, and an animal has no distaste for exercise. We all like companionship, if not intercourse, and speech is, as it were, the fare we pay for transportation in the common vehicle. We love to frame occasions in which it is imperative that certain things should be said but not in the least necessary that they should be either thought or felt.

Consciousness, then, is a laggard. Its backwardness may be shown in four ways. A man may say the opposite of what he thinks and feels; that begets the swindling, lying, and hypocrisy so general in commerce, politics, and sex. The man may feel and think as he speaks, but less, often far less, intensely; that is the exaggeration so common in religion, in the cult of the arts, in the official utterances of states or academic institutions, where, indeed, too often nothing is felt but the obligation to pretend to feel. This leads to the third phase, where the words are uttered without any interior "Yes" or "No" on the speaker's part; this is mechanism, so widespread in education. Lastly, the feeling itself as a vent for temperament may be actual enough, but the choice of its object is conventional — a condition so frequent in sports, in accomplishments, in theatrical and literary vogue, where interest is at once obedient and eager, like a hunting dog.

There are two medicaments for this disparity between the poverty of the internal fact and the opulence of the external symbol; they may be called the ways of faith and of knowledge. Faith assumes a reality behind the sign. Without stooping to the vulgar credulity which provides livelihoods for the beggar, the advertiser, and the swindler, it assumes the validity of the undisproved or undiscredited appearance. Faith accepts the *check* as proof of the *balance*. It assumes that, if a thousand people are drawn to a church on Sunday evening, their motives are religious. Why not? If a thousand people are drawn to a restaurant on Sunday evening, does anybody doubt that their motives are alimentary? The believers assume that, when a crowd cheers, the cheerers at least are enthusiastic. They believe that patriotism is an enduring fire in the heart, not a spark evoked by the collision of surfaces. If a play has swept the country, it is supposed that the joy felt by the last person in the top gallery in Los Angeles is consubstantial with the joy felt by the play's earliest discoverer in New York. It is forgotten that a crowd loves another crowd; that crowds, like individuals, are gregarious. These men assume education in the educated; they impute compassion to philanthropists. They believe that experience is the forerunner of expression, though they might learn from their children that it is easier to say "Thank you" than to be grateful, and that, in the order of tuition, the easier exercise comes first.

This type of mind, at its best, is high and useful. Its possessors believe that others mean what others say, and this is proof of two good things: first, that *they* mean what *they* say, and, second, that they think other men as good as they are; in a word, they are sincere and fraternal. They can often mold men; we mold only what we love. They face the wrongdoer with that genuine surprise at evil which denounces more strongly than denunciation. They often impose their estimate of a man upon the man himself; he values his own character less than its reflected and exalted image in the glass of their intelligence. Ingenuous in a sort they are, but theirs is the kind of guilelessness whose company the insights and the perspicacities delight in.

Admirable as they are, they cannot quite protect themselves from satire. We are ready in our peevishness to declare that, if they gain the end of life, they miss its point, and there are minds for whom the point exceeds the end in interest if not in value. The point is this: that life, on the side of consciousness, is a form that is turning into a fact, a make-believe that is headed for reality. First, the physical deed; second, the intellectual and spiritual appearance; third, the intellectual and spiritual reality. This order is natural in a species which invents courtesy because it is not strong enough to love its neighbor, invents decency because it lacks the vigor to be chaste, makes worship the parent — not the child — of reverence, and adopts a religion the inward experience of which has failed in nineteen hundred years to overtake its precepts. The goal of sincerity, viewed in the historic panorama, is less to make men say what they think and feel than to make men think and feel what they do and say. There is a point of view from which the whole pathos, the whole drama and poetry, of life spring from the rare and unforeseeable emergence of the real, in spots and grains, from the glittering and shallow levels of pretense. Shams are intrinsically vulgar, but spiritual man, even when a sham, is not vulgar, because his is a slowly and imperfectly self-expelling, self-repudiating lie. That is why I find the highest and most moving symbolism in current drama in Percy MacKaye's *Scarecrow,* wherein the old Hawthornesque Feathertop, the frame of rags and sticks, strives to be man, puts on and lays off a fitful humanity as the coals in his life-bestowing pipe are kindled or expire.

I proceed to illustrate the meaning of this view of life by the forms which it assumes in half a dozen fields of thought and action.

Emerson, in a list of people who attended his London lectures in 1848, instances Jane Carlyle and Mrs. Bancroft, "who honestly come." Many come, but few *honestly* come to all largely attended lectures. Men of high vitality have no conception of the paucity or penury of motive that suffices to draw the unoccupied and resourceless man into a popular assembly. Yet almost any speaker knows that, just as an audience finds its *mouthpiece* in the man who speaks well, it finds its *earpiece* in the few or in the one who listens perfectly. Let these ears vanish, and for the speaker the house, with all its idle feint of plethora, is depopulated. Attendance is so much simpler than attention; the body is fonder of travel than the mind. Every teacher feels that his discourse is fulfilled, is born, as it were, in the few minds whose presence in the classroom is an unqualified reality.

This rarity of the true appreciation is illustrated even in laughter, the enjoyment of which appears to be so peculiarly spontaneous and universal. It is quite true that the demonstration, after the fashion of demonstrations, tends to expand, and that everybody who takes part feels a certain pleasure. But most of this is simple resonance; the good joke in its breadth and succulence is the property of the few, and the enjoyment of the others is convivial. The success of a platform or stage joke is often determined by the initiative of a few hearers, not rarely by the leadership of one. There are people whose laughter at a joke is a larger fact in human history than the joke itself. They *own* the jest; the test of proprietorship is appropriation. The truth is that the sense of humor, in any vital form, is far rarer than the taste for collective joviality.

But the same thing is true of that wider and less visible audience which consumes books. Reading — the travel of the eyes across or down a page — is a facile exercise; but readership, in its full sense, is a high function, a high accomplishment, and (to the author) a high service. Robert Browning said of his wife's *Aurora Leigh,* "I wish I had written it and she had read it." Mrs. Browning's authorship had robbed the book of its ideal reader. The author finds this ideal reader inestimable; he is the compatriot met in the foreign country; the true royalties are a few discerningly enthusiastic notes. The esteem for criticism, which persists so indomitably through all the abuse of criticism, springs from the original identification of the critic with this appointed — not to say anointed — reader. The depressing fact is that right readers among critics are few because criticism makes a trade of reading, and the trader simply cannot read.

With cults and gospels it is much the same. Jesus,

in the pressure of a throng, perceived that virtue *in a solitary instance* had gone out of him. The touches, the pressures, were many; the passage of virtue was exceptional. In a modern church real piety distinguishes the believer not among worldlings merely but among the faithful; it confers distinction even on a preacher. Piety is internal; zeal, which relates mainly to conduct, is less unusual among laymen, and is not infrequent in the pulpit. Men are active and sociable; it is not hard to get them together, to obtain their co-operation in acts and words of which the present cost is small and the future dividends (presumably) are enormous. The hard thing is to make them think and feel. Fifty years ago in the evangelical Protestant churches evidence was required that something definite and interesting had taken place in the heart and mind of the prospective member. Today the requirement has virtually lapsed; the church gives up the exaction of the unobtainable; admission is simplified to a degree which includes practically no demands upon the emotions or the intellect. Yet experience is still possible, still discoverable, and the faithful, who deny its peculiarity, perceive and respect its distinction. Oddly enough, the few persons who actually " live by aspiration, hope, and love " never perceive their own rarity; still less do they grasp the futile and ignominious abeyance into which their presence sweeps the companions with whom they mix in joyful and confiding fellowship.

Patriotism might seem, at the first glance, to stand upon another basis. A country has no difficulty in getting people to shout for her on anniversaries, and surprisingly little, it must be confessed, in getting people to die for her on battlefields. Secure at once of the manifestation and the results, it is excusable for not troubling itself about the mental experience that underlies — or fails to underlie — these cheering symptoms. The observer may proceed a little further. No passion of nominally equal force is so little dwelt upon in literature, and the reason is plain; the psychology of patriotism is confined and elementary. Its restriction to occasions is remarkable. No man is ever caught loving his country. Is a man a patriot in the solitude of his bed at midnight? Is a country ever simply, silently, undemonstratively, loved? Why do we pause, almost in wonder, when Wordsworth talks of feeling for his country "like a lover or a child"? By the simplest, sharpest, and most conclusive of tests, the frequency of the recurrence of the loved image to the mind, nations are not loved by loyal citizens. In Barbusse's *Under Fire* the setting is military, the author is a skillful and sympathetic analyst of the psychology of a French *poilu*. The French are renowned for patriotism, and the book scarcely records a patriotic feeling. The reason why we institute Fourths and Fourteenths of July is not that our feelings clamor for expression, but that we hope that occasions may beget expressions and that expression may produce feeling.

I am not decrying patriotism; I am simply pointing out that in most men acts and words rather than emotions are its groundwork.

It is hard to interest people; interest is a form of feeling, and a race of active sinews and drowsy mind feels with difficulty. Everybody knows how eager a theatrical audience is to be pleased, and how hard it is to please them. In the contemplation of great works of art the conditions are superlatively favorable; the object of the work is emotion, the observer is eager to be moved, and the force behind the enterprise is genius. Yet how few are the moments when great art arouses even in qualified recipients the degree of emotion which, to borrow an illustration from Mr. Shaw, is produced in a woman of fifty by the arrival of the postman! We have no difficulty in remembering our vividly happy moments in art galleries; they are so few that their carriage is no burden to the memory. Byron, in a passage of memorable sharpness, complains that only a small fraction of the work of master poets is even good. Shift the target from their feebleness to our apathy, and the censure is not very far from just. Everybody who has watched even a fairly cultivated musical audience has been invited to observe that its keenest satisfactions occur not in the moments when it is absorbing melody but in the moments when it is producing hubbub. The applause in which a languid audience recovers its vitality is prompted as much by gratitude for the cessation of the divine stream as by eagerness for its renewal.

I have no wish to be cheaply cynical at the expense of the clientele of any art. I wish to show that, just as only one client in fifty genuinely sees or reads or listens, so it is only at intervals and at long intervals that even this favored customer really and thoroughly performs his part. I observe that any large section of music — an art to which I am largely impervious — or of poetry — an art to which I am distinctly sensitive — is enjoyed by me in such a fashion that a " hand's breadth of it shines alone in the blank miles round about." In poetry, in music, in painting and sculpture, even in the ruder theater, our pleasure takes the form of a few rare, unforetold, and vanishing fulfillments with interspaces on which the wayward, bright, evasive possibility sheds its gleam. In a word, our contemplation of all these arts is mainly prescience, retrospect, assumption; the entrance of reality, i. e., of vital experience, is the quickening and powerful exception.

Lovers, when apart, count the weeks, and finally the days, of separation; when together, they count the flitting seconds of their tryst. It might be thought that here, if anywhere, reality was constant, and hope and effort vanished in fruition. The truth is probably this: the longed-for interview which is their goal is the beginning of a new quest; the priceless moment in the priceless interview must now be sought. The whole secret is revealed in the few words which I italicize in one of Mrs. Browning's *Sonnets from the Portuguese:*

>   a trick of thought
> That falls in well with mine, and certes brought
> A sense of pleasant ease *on such a day.*

"On such a day." The perfect moments even in a love
like the Brownings' can be picked out; they are datable.
Of course the possibility enlivened the entire meeting.
A gamester's whole afternoon is vivified by the prospect or the mere chance of one exceptionally lucky
throw. Figure ordinary acquaintance as sea level, and
love is mainly a broad plateau broken by a few sky-
grazing peaks. It is something to have the peaks for
neighbors.

Any man, looking back upon the history of unbroken and continuously helpful friendships, is lucky
if he can recall half a dozen moments when feeling
reached a point which corresponded to his own enduring estimate of the worth of the relation. I remember an occasion in a common shop when in twenty
seconds, in the execution of a featureless commercial
act, a friendship that I had cherished for years suddenly
reached its unannounced, and possibly its unreturning,
flower. Even in parenthood, and more especially in
motherhood, where feeling keeps a higher level and
rises to more frequent culminations, the soundness of
the principle is verified. Emotion is largely an effect
of leisure, and may be swept temporarily aside by the
very exertions which its energy has prompted. The
emphasis on partings and meetings is well judged;
the hope is that the jar of breaking or renewing con-

tacts may coax that anchorite, the perfect moment, from its cell.

We come, finally, to life itself. Life is a *function,* a series of acts, a series which is unbroken while life lasts. But life is also a feeling; we feel ourselves to be alive. Theoretically, the feeling should be coextensive with the series; practically, the sense of life, the grasp of its fullness and its value, is so rare as to constitute an occurrence, almost an event. There is a remark by a character in Ibsen's *Lady from the Sea* that I have often paused to consider wonderingly, so far removed is it from all that observation and experience have taught me. Arnholm thinks that most people take life "with a great, calm, unconscious joy." That ought indeed to be the continuous feeling of the recipients of the unequaled boon of life, a privilege beside which kingship and genius are trivialities. But in the real world we need no Tennyson to tell us, " 'Tis life whereof our nerves are scant . . . more life and fuller that we want."

It sometimes seems as if only the imminence of death could make our sense of life commensurate with our sober and dispassionate opinion of its value; the two extremes of life, birth and death, when seen in others, help us, like all beginnings and endings, to realize the worth and force that continuity has blunted. We borrow life from drugs, as we borrow money from the Jews; insolvency is the outcome in both cases. Even the highest life is subject to the same restriction. The space between Saturday nights is long for the drinking navvy, and the interval between Sinai and Nebo is long for the servant and companion of Jehovah.

The situation may be formulated thus. Man is primarily a contrivance for action; feeling and thought are largely episodic; he thinks when he must and feels when he can. On the animal or selfish plane psychic experience *en bloc* is not impracticable. But on any higher level, reality in psychical experience is infrequent, transitory, and particular. Quality in the inner life is the property of the few and even of the rarer moments of the few. This truth is curiously masked by the circumstance that the ministry to the higher being is largely organized on an assumption that directly contradicts this principle — on the assumption, to be precise, that these benefits may be *general* and *continuous*. The lecture, the book, the concert, the tour of the gallery, the conversation, the lovers' rendezvous, the act of worship (if we do worship), are all blocks, are all based on the assumption that vivid experience on a high level may be consecutive. Several of the forenamed ministries are based on the further assumption that experience of this kind can be grasped by assemblies. Hence the true quality of this experience, its rarity, its strangeness, its unexpectedness, its provocative and wayward charm, is hidden from us by the breadth and system of its apparatus.

Words, deeds, and the lower feelings may be systematized; the higher feelings hold rebelliously aloof. Hence every institution of ideal aim which operates on a large scale in space or time becomes futile when it talks. Denunciation of this natural result is likewise futile; the nature of things may be harmful but is never guilty. Matter is an old hand at its game, and its performance is at least respectable; consciousness is a bungler, because it is an apprentice, and the bunglings of apprenticeship are forgivable. The vain sonorities which emanate from patriotic, academic, and religious gatherings should be viewed less as hollow vaunts than as signals pointing consciousness to its destination. There remains, further, the power of real feeling at any moment—for a moment—to restore institutions and rituals to their lost reality and vigor. A church, for instance, may be profitably looked at as a chance for somebody here and there, for somebody now and then, to reach a profound and consecrating moment.

Our preachers, even our wiser and better preachers, are incessantly harping on the battle between weak flesh and willing spirit, on the gulf between high insight and low performance. Ibsen himself tells us, in words exalted enough for Isaiah, to "live the vision into deed." All this is mainly sound and wise, but there is another moral, rare even on prophetic lips, which has an equal title to homage and obedience — to live the deed into vision. We are better than our acts? Sometimes; but our acts are often better than our minds. Most grown people work, and most work is helpful to others; yet consciousness in this humane and Christian exercise is mainly busy with the benefit to self. Our acts are sometimes goals toward which our thoughts are climbers. Schiller, almost forgotten in America, still holds lessons which a thoughtless hemisphere might fitly ponder.

> Das ist's ja, was den Menschen zieret,
> Und dazu ward ihm der Verstand,
> Dass er im innern Herzen spüret,
> Was er erschafft mit seiner Hand.
> —*Das Lied von der Glocke*

I spoke earlier in this essay of a high class of persons whose attitude toward human nature is one of sympathetic faith and friendliness, persons whose habit is to find reality in every undiscredited appearance. They assume the *general* sincerity of mankind, and therefore the *general* validity of favorable manifestations. They see excellence in lines; I look for it in dots. Of the two views neither perhaps is true enough to have the right to call the other false. Just now my wish is to compare, not their soundness, but the shape and color which they give to life. There is a pleasure in the bird song, the "continuous and unbroken strain." There is another pleasure of slighter ground, but of equal force and subtler quality, in the bird call, when, intermittently, the singer from the brakes "starts into voice a moment, then is still." The people who prefer the second, many or few, are the persons whose letters or whose verses one would like to read. Another comparison involves the same truth. A steady moon in a clear sky is a beautiful object, a comforting and guiding object; but there is a peculiar charm in a clear but moonless November night in which expectation vibrates round the possibility that at any moment sky and earth may be lit by the brief refulgence of a falling meteor. Such is the lot of him who, amid a world of forms and shams and mechanisms and vacuities, awaits, not too confidently, the flash of unheralded reality and watches, not too regretfully or repiningly, the reabsorption of that brightness by the gloom. Sincerity is everlastingly possible, and possibility has its own exhilarations. There is no screen that we draw, there is no gate that we enter, there is no stair that we mount, beyond which the coy reality may not wait with a shy welcome in its unaverted eyes.

There are two opposing tendencies in the world, a movement from appearance toward reality, and a countermovement back from reality into appearance. Where the life-current is accelerating, as in childhood, the semblance is converted into fact; where the current slackens, as we see in old age, and emphatically in the case of Polonius, what had been experience hardens into form. In the symbolic transformations of their affluent mythology the Greeks did not fail to include both the Niobe in whom the woman congeals into statue and the Galatea in whom the image quickens into life. Which the universe prefers we cannot know; it is doubtful if it holds a preference for either. But our own choice is firm and irrevocable. We wait, we watch, we hope; the hours are not all untender; sincerity will yet revisit us. In the long interim of expectation we tell ourselves and each other that, if the secret treasure has a lock, it has a key.

THE ETHICS OF TASTE

In AUTHORSHIP the writer's self is a very bad place of abode, but may be an excellent point of departure, especially if the departure be prompt. I shall not apologize for beginning my remarks on the ethics of taste by pointing out a difference in my attitude toward two arts to both of which as critic I am closely, if menially, related. In one of these arts I respond to the best, but am unmindful, am often intolerant and impatient, of anything that falls short of the best. I like a very few things very much; the rest I scarcely like at all. In the second art I am eager for the best, but the art itself, the form, is so dear to me that I can take pleasure in its second-rate, its third-rate, and its fourth-rate manifestations. I am so abandoned or so privileged — let the reader say which — that I can enjoy this art when it is empty, when it is silly, or when it is stale.

In the first art I discriminate and reject; in the second I discriminate, but include. Most people would feel perhaps that the dignified, reputable, and commanding attitude was the first, but that the human, healthy, and genial attitude was the second. The same person might be proud of exclusiveness and glad in hospitality. But the day might come when he would ask himself why all the honors should go to exclusive-

ness, when all the profits go to inclusiveness plus discrimination. He might even proceed to ask whether
that resonant and conquering phrase "love of the best"
were not a stratagem for casting upon the object the
blame for the starved subject's incapacity for love.

Let us try a bit of Socratic dialogue. The questioner
addresses a man who objects to the second-rate in
poetry. Is it good to love Shakespeare and Milton? —
By all means. Loving Shakespeare and Milton, is it
well to love Tennyson and Keats? — Assuredly. Loving
Tennyson and Keats, is it good to love Byron and
Scott? — Undoubtedly. Loving Byron and Scott, is it
wise to love Hood and Austin Dobson? — Probably.
Loving Hood and Dobson, should we gain by a taste
for James Whitcomb Riley or Eugene Field? — Perhaps. At what point in the descent would it become a
virtue to cease to enjoy? At Mrs. Hemans? At Mrs.
Sigourney? At Mrs. Wilcox? Does the virtue cease
when the defects exceed the merits? — Undoubtedly;
but the enjoyment of a form presupposes that, for the
enjoyer, the merits overcome the defects.

Morals apart (and morals are not here in question)
it would seem that the limit to rightness in enjoyment
is the limit to enjoyment itself. In art what can please
should please. The relation of a wooden line like Gas-
coigne's "When thatchers think their wages worth
their work" to "Absent thee from felicity awhile" is
not the relation of a bad penny to a good one but the
relation of a good penny to a thousand-dollar bill.

Every verse that will scan has a grain of merit. A man is fortunate in the power to enjoy that merit. Whether he should give his time to the order of verse in which that merit is predominant or peculiar is another question, depending on the width and worth of his alternatives. The scholar has richer alternatives; for him enjoyments of the kind, though legitimate, might be thriftless. For the yokel they might be both legitimate and paying, and the scholar who sneered at the yokel would lessen and cheapen himself in the act.

In fact, criticism, if its diction were philosophical, would often say "more" or "less," where it now says "good" or "bad." "Bad" is a clumsy term to denote the maladjustment of certain forms of art to particular classes in whom the sensibilities which those forms ignore have been conspicuously, often artificially, developed.

The actual attitude of taste is very far from disclosing this humane and liberal tolerance. It is not content to avoid the undesirable; it is not content to warn its clients of the insufficiency of certain objects for their purpose. It wishes to *brand* the undesirable; it wishes to punish it; it would be glad, apparently, to expel it from the world. The vocabulary which it employs, "tawdry," "loud," "vulgar," "flashy," "stale," "pinchbeck," "raw," "mawkish," is the vocabulary of insult. Its conduct may be set forth in a supposition. Imagine the invasion and occupation of our planet by a race of beings to whose more sensitive and rarefied mold

Shakespeare seemed savage and Raphael mushy. They live with us as the French live with the Algerians or the Americans with the Filipinos. Even in a world remodeled by their presence, *The Merchant of Venice* and the Sistine Madonna would doubtless hold their place and primacy among the ministers of good and joy to us. Would these supermen serve the world or us, would their conduct be humane and generous, would it be even decent or just, if they darkened and defiled in our eyes the sources of our pleasure and well-being?

That, nevertheless, is the exact and proper image of the behavior of the higher taste toward the lower in the field of actuality. A bar, sometimes a ban, is placed between men and the esthetic food which their culture in a specific art inclines them to enjoy. What is the result? They may forego these enjoyments. They may enjoy defiantly. Or, again, they may enjoy cringingly and covertly, after the fashion of boys who betake themselves to the stable or the wood-lot for the absorption of the forbidden cigarette. Either feeling, furtiveness or defiance, is foreign to the amenity and serenity which are the seemly and natural accompaniments of esthetic pleasure. The difficulty is heightened by the fact that the same man's taste in three several arts may act on three distinct and widely parted levels. A man who has the taste of a Shelley in literature may have the taste of a broker in painting and the taste of an Iroquois in music. His attainments admit him to the society of people who keep him abject and writhing on the score of his limitations. Taste is a maker of outcasts. The simple truths that the education of mankind in esthetics is carried forward on many planes and that the primer is just as respectable as the second or sixth reader, though it is not useful to the same persons, are truths beyond its capacity to grasp.

The arrogance of taste is almost universal, and its cruelty in former times often rivaled its arrogance. Criticism has been historically a savage art, and the last century has tamed its manners without sapping its faith in the necessity and sanctity of its judgments. Amy Lowell, in her very interesting review of Vachel Lindsay's *The Golden Whales of California,* is as inexorable in the enforcement of a standard as Poe in his mingled diatribe and glorification of Elizabeth Barrett Browning. Radicalism is as exigent in its own fashion as conservatism. Its hatred of the banal, that is to say, of the sin of getting good from a thing that has been fertile in good to thousands or myriads of your predecessors, is religious in its depth and superstitious in its nicety. Taste in any school falls into the oddest inconsistencies. For instance, one of its most perennial manifestations is an intense hostility to every form of self-display or self-complacence. Now, to make the expression of self-consciousness a crime in a being in whom the dominance of self-consciousness is practically continuous is in effect to put a ban upon sincerity. Taste will not let us pretend to be what we are not;

that is an enormity known as affectation. But, having laid down this salutary law, it turns around and insists upon our exhibition of the monstrous and grotesque pretense that we are totally indifferent to ourselves.

I am not condemning taste for this particular inconsistency; there is often much reason in a stand in which there is very little logic. My general assumption, indeed, in the present argument is that taste is valid — in other words, that it prefers the preferable. This concession I am in no way bound to make, since the gravity and frequency of its errors are notorious. But my immediate quarrel with taste is on another score. I am not questioning its verdicts; I question its penalties. I object to the disgrace and odium which it is allowed to heap upon the rebels to its law. The relation of the tasteless to the tasteful man, in my judgment, is not that of the Samaritan to the Jew or the pagan to the Christian, but that of the deacon to the priest. Taste is a persecutor; that is its prime error and offense; that would remain its prime error and offense if every tenet of its creed were found to be impregnable.

The most powerful of all examples is our own, and it is fortunate for our groping race that in two points, possibly in three, it has found its way to ideally right conduct in this dubious affair of taste. The first of these is our attitude toward the rude attempts of early savages to express a feeling for beauty in material things. An approach to straightness in the blade of a humble weapon, the intimation of a curve in a handle, a rude cutting here and there on a rebellious surface, are viewed by us with a feeling in which reverence unites with pity. We watch with tenderness, with piety, the young race putting its timid foot on the first step of that noble stair at the summit of which wait Dante, Phidias, and Shakespeare. A single plastic line in early sculpture, a single fluid line in early verse, is rife with prophecies that touch us to the quick. The second form of ideal rightness in our critical attitude is the warmth of our reception to the faintest outbreak of vision or melody in the drawings, rhymes, or trilling of young children. Our own attitude toward our childish tastes participates in this humanity. Every cultivated man recalls the vivid response of his own childhood to verses of which his maturer judgment distrusts the worth or proclaims the worthlessness. Many instances prove (two, in my very recent reading, from Edmund Gosse and Jules Lemaître, come back to me with signal vividness) that he treasures the experience, whatever the effect of re-perusal and reappraisal may have had on his judgment of the merit of the verses. Suppose that my neighbor's taste at forty agrees with my own in boyhood. My bearing toward the little ranter or sentimentalist that I chanced to be at ten or fifteen years should surely instruct me in the fitting attitude toward people in whom the love of rant or sentiment has survived the advent of hair to the chin or its departure from the cranium.

A third illustration might possibly be drawn from

our sympathy with the foreign student's attitude toward the tritenesses and flatnesses of our language. For that student, the commonplace in our tongue does not exist. The new word burnishes the dingy object. In one of the early novels of William Black a German lieutenant is the fellow traveler of two English women. The women laugh at a vapid song, "Flow on, Thou Shining River." The lieutenant says (in substance), "That is poetry to me. The river *flows* and it *shines*." Surely the lieutenant's view was sound. A person for whom a line is a picture is undoubtedly better off than a person for whom it is a mere buzz in the ear. But if an Englishman, not a German, had found the picture in the line, the women would have thought him silly. In other words, an Englishman is a fool for seeing in his own language the glance and sparkle which is apparent to a foreigner. Paradox could go no further.

But we are tired of such phrases. Certainly we are tired. But where, outside of art, would anyone affirm or assume that satiety was judicial? Yet what are all these denunciations of words and thoughts as threadbare or stale or banal, verdicts pronounced with such rare gusto and accepted with such pious meekness, but the verdicts of satiety?

I wish now to make a little clearer the nature of these affections for supposedly unworthy objects to which taste is so ready to apply the whip or the brand.

Señor Blasco Ibañez, in his vivid journalistic reports from Mexico, told us that the face of Carranza was imposing. He instantly qualified this praise by adding that the effect of majesty was largely impaired by a single unlucky feature, a large, thickly veined, and deeply colored nose. He qualified this qualification by adding that from a distance the defects of the nose were imperceptible. From these facts flow one or two obvious consequences. A man shaking hands with Carranza might have refused to see majesty in his face. A man viewing his face across the breadth of a public square might have decided instantly that it was ma-jestic. The two judgments would both be in a sense correct; they might spring from identical standards; the difference might be so purely circumstantial that an exchange of locations would induce an exchange of views. In the same way the judgment that an actress is beautiful may be perfectly sound from the twenty-fifth row of the orchestra; from the second row it may be ludicrous.

The illustration may be modified in a way that will greatly increase its aptness for my purpose. Let us sup-pose that the two spectators sit side by side, but that the one has normal vision, the other is short-sighted, sees much less distinctly, or, in other words, sees much less. He does not perceive the defects which injure or ruin the face for his companion; he calls it beautiful. Now this is an ignorant judgment, but—granting the ignorance—it is not a foolish, nor even a false, judg-ment. What is seen is beautiful; only much less is seen. Now, my theory is simply that the tasteless person is the short-sighted person. He views the object from a distance — in his case organic rather than linear — at which the defects that offend the nearer or keener person are unperceived.

Why is a bad picture admired? No picture which finds a buyer or a spectator is without a few lines or tints in which some neighborship with truth, some friendliness with beauty, is revealed. What the bad judge loves in the bad picture is these approaches. He loves the good in the bad. His defect lies in the arrest of his vision at a few bold details upon the surface; the rest is unobserved or unheeded. The bad observer's relation to the picture is that of the man who has read only the first chapter of a book, and found the first chapter interesting. The person who has followed that hopeless book through its vapid middle to its inept conclusion may have the right to call this observer superficial, indolent, or uninformed, but he has no right to say that the observer likes evil.

The same law is exemplified in those imitations or restorations of Gothic which repel a cultivated taste while they attract the untutored eye. The untutored eye gets no further than those aspects in which the imitation or the restoration is successful. It halts before the infamies begin.

We do no justice to the amount of truth in works which are supposed to reek with falsity. Imagine a visitor — not a man — from the nebula of Orion who should spend two hours at a moving picture show on the night of his arrival on this planet. He would acquire a vast deal of profitable truth. He would learn something about dress and housing, about streets and cities, about riches and labor, about law and crime, about men and women, about courtship and marriage, about parents and children, about suffering and death. It is doubtful if he would double his knowledge by going the next night to see *Hamlet*. This is nothing against Shakespeare, who was not writing a handbook for immigrants, but is a point in favor, or in palliation, of the cinematograph. Let us try to be clear and just. The people who go to these films, though they love many lies, do not hate truth. On the contrary, they love truth; only, like Coleridge, like Matthew Arnold, like every sensible man who ever read a novel or saw a play, they want truths that are on a level with their perceptions. Their perceptions are circumscribed, undoubtedly; they are short-sighted; that is all the trouble.

I have tried to show in these last pages that the tasteful and the tasteless perception agree in direction even when they differ in material. A reference to the law of attention will help to clarify this point.

Dr. Johnson had a blind housekeeper. When the lady poured tea for Dr. Johnson and his guests, she tested the fullness of the cups by the insertion of her finger in the liquid. The eighteenth century could drink this tea; the twentieth century can hardly stomach it even in anecdote. The difference is a matter of attention. Dr. Johnson and his friends ignored the finger. We *heed* nothing else. Are we right? If to our scorn of the tea we add a scorn of the tea drinkers, we are certainly wrong. The warmth, the stimulus, the flavor, of the tea were unimpaired by the contact with the finger, and these are the relevant points in tea; the finger, on which we obstinately fix our minds, is the irrelevance. Nobody can be rightly despised, nobody can be called guilty, for concentrating his mind upon essentials.

What troubles me in this peremptory condemnation is that the warmth, the stimulus, the flavor, of the defiled tea are as nothing in the eyes, or mouth, of taste. Taste does not weigh these things against the finger in the judicial balance; the moment her eye lights on that finger, she flings her balances out of the window. Her conduct is precisely like that of Petruchio in *The Taming of the Shrew,* who, having found matter for objection in a particular dish, flings the plates right and left in contempt of the remaining viands. Taste is the insulted man who becomes on the instant stone-blind to the most obvious talents and virtues of the insulter. The object seen by taste in these movements of wrath is not the real object, but a contrivance, a fabrication, a bogy. It is made by the method proper to malicious caricature, the exaggeration of one or two evil traits accompanied by the effacement or defacement of all the lovable or pleasing qualities. Taste, having created this monster, endeavors to persuade itself and others that this is the creature which bad taste loves. Bad taste loves nothing of the kind. Bad taste would fly from the deformity, as the base mechanicals in *A Midsummer Night's Dream* fled from the ass's head in which the mockery of more delicate spirits had disguised the natural homeliness of their old comrade Bottom. What it loves is a quite different object, an object created out of the same thing by a transfer of attention to its more genial and winning traits.

At this point we face a pertinent question. What is the justification of taste? What is the gain that warrants men in the setting up of an authority which debars them from so many joys? The case of Dickens' mawkish pathos supplies us with an answer. What taste seeks in branding the Dickensian pathos as mawkish is to establish a standard that will enable us, in the higher literature at least, to obtain a pathos from which this taint of mawkishness is purged away. Let us glance at one consequence of this process.

The end is high, but the end is disciplinary; and discipline, when efficient, is usually illiberal, intolerant, cantankerous, and niggling. Every schoolmaster who wishes to control practice must be, or feign to be, a fanatic in order to obtain even that modest level of proficiency which temperate and balanced reason would approve. The only good teachers of English are the teachers in whom the insistence on correctness in language approaches a mania. Manners are certainly not puerilities, but nobody can impress decorums on a stubborn race without an emphasis on niceties which is puerile. Taste has the same difficulties. It never triumphs. It is always carrying on a battle with tastelessness in which the opponent is formidable and the victory unsure. Its ethics are the unscrupulous ethics of war. It is in danger; it is in terror; its fear makes it unjust; and its injustice makes it libelous. In other words, it tells lies about the enemy. It feels that it has nothing to fear from the child or the savage, and its attitude toward their experiments is liberal, catholic, and humane. But in the culture that adjoins and underlies its own, it divines a claimant for its place, and it turns with jealous truculence upon its rival. The highest mind is that in which taste is so secure that it can dare to perceive in the things which it once impugned and rejected parts of that world-wide and age-long movement toward beauty of which its own excellence is the temporary crown. Let it so humanely and wisely deport itself that it may plead its mercy to yesterday when it stands at the bar of tomorrow.

I come back to the point from which I set out — the art in which I am capable of joy on many planes — with an increased faith in the righteousness of my pleasure. Fastidiousness may well be a transitional state, a state of insecurity, in which special dikes and defenses are imperative to avert the threatened reflux of the barbaric flood. But I remember that "fastidiousness" has affinities with "loathing," and that even the far nobler word "discrimination" is haunted by a

shadow of "crime." To the humane and liberal eye
the search for beauty everywhere is beautiful, and the
kindness flowing out toward child and savage will
not seal its founts to philistine or bourgeois. One may
love an art to the point when its very levities and littleness shall become dear to us, like the whims and
follies of a beloved child. It is pleasant to live life
simultaneously on many stages. The father of three
boys will take the eight-year-old to the pantomime, the
twelve-year-old to *Monte Cristo,* and the sixteen-year-
old to *Secret Service,* with a sympathy that involves no
peril to his loyalty to Sophocles or Ibsen. Would the
pleasure be less valuable or palatable if the occasions
had been not three sons, but three moods? In an art
which operates on many levels it is a pity that pleasure
should frequent only one; in a world where the best is
exceptional, he is poor who is confined to the best.
The ethics of taste tend finally to an appreciativeness
which shall be at the same time as high as the best
and as broad as the good.

UNDEPICTED AMERICA

TWENTIETH-CENTURY America is a fact among many like facts, a unit in a comprehensive and assimilative whole. Nineteenth-century America was a fact by itself, had its unshared and unprized peculiarity. That peculiarity is caught and held in an anecdote that skirts the life of Emerson. A caller on Sarah Alden Ripley found her engaged at one time in four whimsically divergent occupations. She was teaching calculus to a Harvard student; she was correcting another Harvard student's translation of Sophocles; she was shelling peas; and her foot rocked from time to time the baby's cradle. Anywhere else this would have been grotesque; nineteenth-century America was the one place where this kind of thing could occur without grotesqueness. In New England at one time two boys on milking stools before cows might have talked of Shakespeare without eccentricity and without fear of satire.

In my childhood my mother, a strong and capable woman, cooked, washed, and ironed for a large family. An education that stopped short at the country school had bred (or spared) in her a taste for sterling poetry, and she worked to the measure of verses which she recited to herself above the kneading bowl or dishpan.

I remember an Italian grammar which she read to her weak-sighted son in the intermissions of a cookery which harvested praises from the most plodding and least lettered of her guests. I ask myself if English cooks and washerwomen did that. Verse has been said (or sung) by workers everywhere, by London house-maids and by Wordsworth's "Solitary Reaper." There is little proof, however, that they chanted or recited literature. My father, a self-taught man, unversed in letters, who brought home copies of Mary J. Holmes's novels, to my mother's unconcealed and forcible disgust, had nevertheless a far-off sense and care for what was true and good in letters. He brought home to his wife and little son one day a secondhand copy of Byron — taken, I half think, in part payment for a bad debt — Byron in one volume in fine print with priceless critical footnotes in a print still more evasively minute. I ask myself whether one of Trollope's bagmen — the bagman in *Orley Farm,* for example — would have bought Byron for his wife and son. I ask myself if a French *commis voyageur* then or now would have done as much for Hugo or Musset, always remembering that it is never safe to say that anything delicately intelligent has not occurred in France.

I have no wish to overstrain the facts. In my state in my youth the ploughman was not expected to know Greek or the brakeman to quote Shakespeare. But the ploughman would have liked his son to know Greek, and the brakeman was proud when his daughter in the high school quoted "To be or not to be" in her commencement essay. The same person might not often be a native or frequenter of both worlds; to both he might easily be neighbor. The difference between rusticity and cultivation was often merely the difference between today and tomorrow. The civilization was on the easiest terms with the natural, the practical, and the homely; and it was on easy terms with the delicate, the intelligent, and the uplifting. The link between the two was a certain simple-heartedness and simple-mindedness. That is what no foreigner and no typical young latter-day American forgives. For my own part, though this is foreign to my point, the more I see of sophistication the more I respect simple-mindedness.

It is easy to see how all this came about. A cultivated people found itself in a primitive setting, taking part in a primitive task. The combination is so desirable that every banker who buys a country seat at the lakeside is pursuing at least the first half of it; but only an accident could make it possible for one member of a block of cultivated states. That accident was the cutting off of half the planet from civilization for centuries by two great oceans. When the oceanic barriers were removed, civilization poured into the waiting basin. The aboriginal setting and the imported tradition, the old time and the new place, acted in common on the settlers, and familiarized man at once with hardy nature and with ideal ends. Social classes were rigid in Europe, fluid in America, and in America the prerogatives and virtues of normally divided classes interflowed.

The classical course affords a timely illustration. In my youth it was still *the* course, the scholar's, the gentleman's course; its associates were not its peers. That belief in America, and especially in western America, had a rare significance — a significance independent of its validity as fact. That Oxford should remember Athens was in the nature of things — Oxford, itself a tradition, Oxford whose vocation was remembrance, Oxford whose spires reach back into the past almost as naturally as they reach up into the blue. But that western America, a civilization still young enough to be casting its forests into its rivers, should actually believe that another civilization beyond the Atlantic and older than Christianity should have lessons and bounties for itself — this showed a meekness that was exquisitely touching. I choose my noun "meekness" and my adjective "touching" with discrimination. Perhaps its faith was like that of devout Catholics in the Mass; but be it remembered that the Mass was at least contemporaneous and visible — a *real presence* in that sense if in no other.

Freedom, again, illustrates the American's inborn peculiarity. The British burgher and yeoman treasured his rights; rights were casings for his person, grates, bolts, and watchdogs for his property. But nobody *worships* bolts or watchdogs. Burke and Wordsworth, in another class, could disenthrall the principle which these securities implied, and worship that. The *value* in England belonged to everybody, the *sanctity* to the elect. Moreover, what in England only the Burkes and Wordsworths and their kind could do was in America, in a sense, within the reach of any decent man. Not all things within everybody's reach are grasped, but the option remains intact and puts its stamp on the community. Our feeling took its key from our Declaration of Independence, and this, in turn, borrowed its key from French ideas which aimed at reverence and exaltation. The ploughman in America spelled Liberty with a capital; in England the habit would have marked a gentleman. These capitals, like other panaches, have been made fun of. But their value is real; they authorize us to hold toward Liberty or Virtue the feelings that we hold toward human beings.

But all this time, if people found companionship in air and fire, they were not less neighborly with the humbler elements, earth and water. The time and place abounded in material solicitations. Ease, of course, was rarely to be had; a continent does not surrender all at once even to Anglo-Saxons. But security, comfort of a sort, and opportunity were general. The soil was liberal and exacting; if it gave freely in harvests, it asked much in labor. You were poor, but you might be rich, and the unique thing was that, if you made the riches moral and intellectual instead of metallic, precisely the same thing was true. Here were good materialities with even better hopes and prospects. Here were good spiritualities, likewise with better hopes and prospects. The coincidence produced a novelty — America.

My point, which is primarily neither moral nor historical, but literary, is twofold. First, this original thing has disappeared, never, apparently, to come again. Second, while it lasted it was never painted. The second point shall be considered first. This unique America of which I speak had two chances — two good chances — to obtain a copy of itself in literature. I am to prove, if I can, that it profited by neither.

The first real chance was the New England group — the men of letters who were born in the first two decades, and died off in the last two decades, of the nineteenth century. Drawing — the means and the faculty — first became obtainable at this time; hitherto America had been merely sharpening its pencil. Very fortunately, though in the end fruitlessly, the springtime of American letters concurred in time with the effloresence of the combination which made America original. Another signal piece of equally useless good luck was the fact that the Emersons, Lowells, and Whittiers were intensely American; none of them were *mere* copyists and cultivators of European manners and ideas.

When I say that these men left America undepicted,

I forbear to add that they left it unvoiced. *Voiced* by
them, in a sense, it undoubtedly was; they were of it,
and its voice was heard in theirs. Emerson indeed, in
a single phrase, has put the whole philosophy of the
movement into six words: "Hitch your wagon to a
star." (It is a most significant little circumstance that
nobody in our time has ventured to bring the precept
up to date by saying: "Hitch your Rolls-Royce to a
star"; there are things that even dullards see to be
impossible.) Lowell, in *The Biglow Papers,* put exactly
the same antislavery sentiments into the mouths of two
men, a punctilious scholar to whom enclitics and Mis-
souri Compromises were equally affecting, and a rough-
handed, strong-hearted son of the soil who trod in the
same couplet upon James K. Polk and Lindley Murray.
Ploughman and scholar were two wrappages for the
same contents. Longfellow writes of "Giotto's Tower"
and of the "Village Blacksmith"; Whittier of the
"Eternal Goodness" and of pumpkin pie (the latter
no unimportant symptom of the former to a true New
Englander). In this vertical range of mere *themes*
there is nothing specifically American — the like can be
found in Wordsworth and even in Tennyson; my point
here is that this doubleness of taste qualified these
writers to see and to depict the synthesis which was the
true originality. Holmes, seeking contacts between culture and vulgarity, plants his "breakfast table" in a
boarding house. Thoreau mixed loam with ideality at
Walden, and Brook Farm was a premature attempt to

turn the fortuitous American combination into an ordinance and a régime which should renovate society.

Why, then, did a group so happily endowed fail to portray America? I am able to specify three reasons of which the first is at the same time the most obvious, the least stimulating, and the most important. Briefly, a great novelist and realist was required, and the New England group, though it met the first of these demands consummately in Hawthorne, was wholly unprepared to meet the second. Hawthorne was a preacher of ethics and psychology in symbols, and was bound over to romanticism by the fact that his favorite symbols shimmered on the wavering edge of possibility. Realism in the mass was impossible to such a mind, and this defection left the group without a spokesman.

The second reason for the failure to depict America lay in the anglophile and cosmophile preoccupations of the clan. I have already said that their temper was American, but they went to England and the Continent just as the housewife, whose life is in her home, goes to market. A nation gets its corn, material or intellectual, where it can, and in this instance the granaries were European. Emerson, for instance, valued both England and America largely as witnesses to the nature of things, and gave priority to England simply as the older and more experienced witness. The attitude of the group *in re* America was not disability or disaffection; the word that fits it best is pre-committal. The day of pupilage was not yet over.

The validity of the third reason which I shall adduce is more debatable, but its interest is hardly matter for debate. The New England movement was largely Unitarian, and Unitarianism, though its scanty membership has included an amazingly large part of what was best and wisest in America, has never been as a sect distinctively or signally American. It reminds one a little of the magnolia in Central Park in New York City. In its time of flower it is almost the most beautiful object in the park and the least indigenous. Unitarianism is an essence, and an essence is not a mixture. It is neither pettily exclusive nor vulgarly disdainful, and it is capable of high sacrifice for the lowly and the downtrodden. Like Milton, it can lay the lowliest duties upon its heart, but the gesture with which it stoops to the burden is Miltonic.

America's primary chance of portraiture was lost. The second chance, though narrower and less outstanding than the first, offered in point of fact the larger promise. Its name was William Dean Howells. He was the meeting-point of many needful or favoring conditions. He was born at a good time, 1837, in a good place, Ohio, material and moral center of the traits which gave a zest to nationality. The son of a needy, migratory editor, who loved books and hated slavery, he was born to privation, to hard work, to idealism, and to letters. To his inbred love of western America, widening experience added the Bostonian and European points of view; he learned to combine affection with objectivity. Moreover, he was, unlike any great member of the earlier group, a realistic novelist, and he wrote novels with an assiduity that amounted to exuberance.

It is hard to say why all these endowments and opportunities failed to do the work, yet somehow, in that beautiful and memorable product, the object of our present search is never quite fulfilled. Howells himself in a lecture once drew a profound distinction between reality and the effect of reality; the latter, he said, was the end of fiction. We might say that his own reality misses a part of its own effect; it convinces without quite persuading; its *authenticity* is a little *unfamiliar*. In my youth my mother once said that my father was unlike any character in fiction. I suggested Silas Lapham. The suggestion was disapproved. " Howells made too much fun of Silas Lapham." Drawing in Lapham a character whom he liked and respected, Howells produced a figure whom an affectionate wife would not willingly identify with her husband. Compare with Trollope, so inferior as a spirit, as an intelligence, to Howells; compare with Tolstoi, the coarser grained, if also the firmer fibered, man. The England or the Russia that these artists drew, if left alone, could get along without them; one has a sense that the guaranteed, the verifiable, America of Howells might disappear if Howells took his hand off. Possibly the people are a little too much judged, tested, assayed; possibly something in Howells shrank, re-

treated, before crudity. Much, very much, stayed behind, admiration, wisdom, observation, sympathy; but
perhaps the thing that fled was the very thing that
consummates the actuality of a portrayal.

The second chance was missed; there was no third.
Whitman drew nothing; he was simply an exclaimer
about Whitman. Mark Twain, whose comedy is largely
definable as a certain fervor and solemnity in impos-
ture, a sheer revelry in humbug, could not stand at
the center of American life; he was " a dancing shape,
an image gay," on its fantastic border. To grasp
America simultaneously by its two handles, aspiration
and practicality, was a task for which the unpractical
and unaspiring Poe was palpably unfit; his settings,
like his temper and his aims, were European. No third
chance could be sought in Henry James or Mrs. Wharton. Europe appropriated Henry James, appropriated
even his pencil; Mrs. Wharton's specialty was that
denationalized, floating aristocracy for whom the Atlantic is not so much an ocean as a strait. The sun of
national idealism had already set before our later (not
our latest) writers, Mr. Dreiser, Mr. Lewis, Mr. Anderson, appeared upon the scene. Not that they could
have seen the orb before it sank; sunset makes no difference to a blind man.

The failure to depict America must not be taken to
mean that regions in the country such as Mr. Cable's
Louisiana or Miss Murfree's eastern Tennessee have not
been duly and vividly portrayed. Whether these de-

lineations satisfy the native as likenesses is a point to be submitted to the Creole and the mountaineer; the general reader, at least, has every right to be content with them as pictures. It may be said that New England is a province with its local chroniclers, and with some claim to the title of spokesman or foreman for the entire country. To this it may be replied that these chroniclers, even when noteworthy, had their special maladjustments. The vigorous and now undervalued Mary Wilkins Freeman steeps all things in the lye of her sardonic temper. Miss Sarah Orne Jewett's New England misses typicality on the other side; it is a rabbit, shy and bright and quiet and demure, a creature to be taken home and made a pet of.

Every chance, then, was thrown away; America eluded portraiture. While the painter was loitering, the model slipped away. America disappeared. The two great elements whose combination had fostered its originality insensibly and rapidly withdrew. These elements, as we have seen, were the primitive setting and the cultivated or ideal tradition.

The year 1929 was the fiftieth anniversary of the appearance of Henry George's *Progress and Poverty*. I have no wish to discuss here the still controversial doctrines of that fearless treatise; it bears on my point simply as one of the earliest proclamations that the idyl of our country — its honeymoon with the virgin continent — was drawing toward a speedy close. We began to see that the European influx was bringing with it an unnamed, unsuspected immigrant, the European problem. Miracle countered miracle; the incredible vastness of the domain found a counterpoise in the incredible swiftness of its appropriation. America had offered to the human race only a transitory relief from a permanent congestion. Mankind had drawn a long breath — a fleeting breath. Whatever was original in the early economic order tended always more certainly and speedily to disappear. The ways, the cramps, the perplexities of Europe took its place.

Almost more swiftly and surely the ideal tradition lost its empire. Darwin published in 1859 the *Origin of Species*. The first blow fell rather on doctrine than idealism. Indeed, for a time the book brought actual help to minds qualified to perceive that a low origin might set off and illumine a high destiny; mankind, like Napoleon, might repel scoffs with *Je suis ancêtre*. Later on, the destiny fell within the shadow of the origin. Virtue lost caste with cultivated persons; from guide, philosopher, and friend, it passed into a convenience — or inconvenience, as the case might be. Then came the World War, in which America and idealism, or its semblance, enlisted together; America won, but idealism lost, that war. Before and after that event the European attitudes, the liberalisms, realisms, estheticisms, and internationalisms, the European distempers, the despondencies and lubricities, filtered or flowed into the American receptacle. Anybody who held up the banner of the ideal became — a Hilmar

Tönnesen. In an American university of our day only one thing could be rarer than a reference in a conversation between two students to a common ground of aspiration; the still rarer thing would be such a reference in the conversation of the faculty. Estimates of this kind often forget the rural population, the surviving *pagus* or paganism in a world dedicated to its own urban type of super-Christianity. But there is no real tenacity or hardihood in this survival; its eagerness to be converted is pathetic. Main Street has read *Main Street,* and falls asleep to dream of Park Avenue.

It is time to remember that the desirability of these changes is distinct from their reality, and that my thesis avers not the desirability but the fact. Believe, if you like, that all these changes are ameliorations; it remains true that they are manifest assimilations, and that, in that aspect, they turn America from its untutored self into a ward or suburb of Cosmopolis. If you object to "ward" or "suburb," call it the public square or forum of Cosmopolis; it has drifted only so much the farther from its primitive distinction. That distinction lay, as we have seen, in the concurrent fellowship with spirit and with matter. Through the lapse of both its elements, that combination has vanished, presumably forever, and, by a curious group of accidents, while it was present it was never drawn.

This does not mean that a great original, realistic novel in America is impossible. Common conditions in two hemispheres no more shut out the possibility of great literature in one hemisphere than in the other. If the American product in the newer vein still falls short of the European, one reason may be that the varnish on our modernity is not dry. America carries her laxities a little stiffly, like a clergyman's son in the pronunciation of his first oath. We are almost too officiously alert; Mr. Sinclair Lewis' mind, for instance, has a likeness to his own typewriter — all briskness, taps, and unsuspended continuity. Mr. Arnold Bennett, a European mind of somewhat kindred stamp, is much more leisurely and self-contained in his exposures. The future may redress these inequalities. What it cannot do is to bring back that vanished America which the contemporary eye and hand were too busy or too negligent to capture. The injury, in any case, is great. Art slept beside its canvas while originality on tiptoe peered in at the door. History has lost a datum, and literature has missed a theme.

HAS EMERSON A FUTURE?

EMERSON in the history of religion was a guest of honor who reached a party at the moment when its members were dispersing. His arrival evoked a brief sensation — on the doorstep, as it were — but did not finally reconstitute the party. In the confusion of dispersal the leading guest found himself for a moment without a shelter or a destination. This is a tiny parable to the consideration of which my thoughts were recalled by the perusal of Mr. Carpenter's scholarly little monograph entitled *Emerson and Asia*.

I

What is Emerson's claim upon the regard of humanity? Restatement in a few words may be instructive even to his admirers.

The association of omnipresence with divinity is an old idea. The association of divinity with worship is an idea still older. Emerson simply saw that, if divinity were omnipresent, the act of worship might be everlasting. The experience of God might be unbroken. The idea was striking; Emerson went much further; he converted the idea into a program. The experiment was audacious — and successful. Emerson's whole secret may be formulated thus: the successful practice of unbroken commerce with omnipresent deity. Or again, in more technical form: the combination of the broadest generality in the religious object with the highest particularity in the continuously varying forms which the object presents to the disciple.

Men had dedicated themselves to God before his day. One class had referred every act to the divine approbation. Another had been professionally devout — had dedicated their whole time to the accumulation of credits in the divine ledger. A few had found in God the object of living: to a few more He had constituted a ground for death. But the notion of an unbroken spiritual commerce which, using every object, should occupy every moment, was a novel thing. Here is a fact that sweeps all the literature and all the intelligence of Emerson, great and moving as these are, into abeyance: here is an addition to history, a new district of experience, an augmentation of the sum of human possibilities. The soundness or unsoundness of the premises on which this principle and this obedience rest is a great matter; but even that greatness is small beside the fact that on any premise, sound or unsound, the result was achievable and was achieved. *"Tant pis pour le sens,"* said Flaubert, when one of his beautifully modulated sentences was charged with defect of sense. If logic and Emerson fail to come to terms, the sufferer is logic.

Two points demand brief notice before we turn to the religious influence of Emerson. His name, let me hasten to say, is secure; he is certain of the due toll of

inscriptions, invocations, appraisements, and obei-
sances — of that form of greeting from posterity which
combines salutation with dismissal. The second point
is that Emerson had two fames, and that the slighter
fame has proved thus far the firmer, more abidingly
dynamic, of the two. This last may be called his secular fame among thinkers. There is no other amateur
to whom so many experts have been grateful. Emerson had the impertinence to say things about politics,
economics, industry, history, and art which the specialists in those fields were generous enough to borrow.

The *Encyclopaedia Britannica* (14th edition) observes tranquilly *in re* Montaigne: "The most noteworthy handling of the subject in English is unquestionably Emerson's in *Representative Men.*" Emerson,
after eighty years, is the first voice in English, not on
the "Over-Soul," but on a French essayist — a fact
visible to encyclopedias! No other man, perhaps, even
today, is so often cited by unaffiliated minds. The Gen-
tiles have been more faithful than straying Israel. An
audience of thinkers, as guarantors of perpetuity, has
the marked advantage of being to a large degree an
audience of spokesmen. What explains this vogue of
the high priest among the unconverted? Many people
would admit that Emerson was the sanest of mystics
because he was the soundest of thinkers, but does it
occur to anybody that he was possibly the first of thinkers because he was the first of mystics? Does anybody
broach the suggestion that the zenith might be the

point from which all levels and all horizons might be most distinctly visible, that the airman might give help to the topographer?

II

I turn now to the larger and nearer question of Emerson's religious influence and destiny. Liberal religion in Emerson's day mounted to a crest from which, shortly after his day, it declined with a swiftness that was almost catastrophe. Emerson gained by the ascent, and furthered the ascent; he lost by the fall which he could not halt, which, indeed, on one side, he was destined indirectly and unwillingly to further. It is a strange and profoundly saddening fact that, in the liberal field, Emerson's peculiar tilth and glebe, faith and worship could hardly be more dim and faint today if their exemplar and evangelist had never lived. The cause of this shall be explored a little later. Let it suffice here to say that Emerson came at the best time possible for a brief, bright ripening of his influence and fame, at the worst time possible for the carrying forward and establishment of these happy prospects. He lost his hold not through any failure in himself and less through any defection or estrangement of his audience than through what we might call its *bodily removal,* as if a man speaking from shore to listeners on a ship were to find his speech cut short by the unmooring and departure of the vessel. The world was adrift from its religious anchorage.

There are times when, comparing the fleetingness

of Emerson's religious influence with the length and
the luster of the trail left by such partial prophets as
Fox and Swedenborg, we are confounded by the stu-
pidity of Time. We must remember, however, that the
carriage of fame, like other carryings, is mainly a question of transports. These transports in religion are doctrines, organizations, rituals, sacraments, programs.
Emerson rejected all these things, as clogs and hindrances to the commerce of the impassioned soul with
vital deity. His fame was a foundling to be laid on
anybody's doorstep. By providence or by luck in one
of its happy mimicries of providence the door at which
the bantling was laid was the door of Unitarianism.
That generous body constituted itself forthwith the
curator of that fame and spiritual efficiency in which it
very justly saw the fruit of its own teaching and the
seed of its own honor. In the wardship of Emerson's
fame, it might well have seemed that it had found its
own security. A Unitarianism anxious for its own future might have been quieted by the word spoken to
the affrighted Roman boatman: *Caesarem vehis, et
fortunam ejus.*

The partnership was more helpful in its beginnings
than later, and tended rather to exalt than to elucidate
the seer. Emerson has often been seen through a blur
of worship. Louisa Alcott as a tiny girl laid violets on
his doorstep, and when in *Rose in Bloom* she made
Emerson almost the matchmaker between two virtuous
young nobodies, she was still in the same uncompre-

hending sincerity strewing violets before his door. Unitarians in general saw much more, but even they tended sometimes to treat Emerson as a jeweler who should give back to them their own thoughts reset in the pearl and gold of his incomparable diction. They saw the unrivaled specimen: they scarcely discerned the *new species.* Emerson, be it remembered, was not their founder or chief; nobody either within or without their body was responsible for Emerson per se, for Emerson in toto. Disciples take en masse: customers — even reverent customers — pick and choose. In Emerson the religious liberals took and left; and these takings and leavings tended to convert the seer into an image, an enlarged and glorified reflection, of themselves.

III

Unitarianism was the product of many influences, the most powerful of which in the mid-nineteenth century was probably Emerson himself. Its tradition was liberal; it drew new fervor and new liberality from Emerson; that was its high fortune. Its misfortune lay in the fact that it lost the fervor while it kept the liberality, and that liberality, in the absence of fervor, is deadly to religion. If, indeed, the ardor does not warm the liberality, the liberality will freeze the ardor. Put in homelier phrase, if the teeth do not break the walnut shell, the walnut shell will crack the teeth. Liberalism is a strain on the vital force of any cult — an ordeal which the Emersons, but not the Emersonians, can

victoriously and profitably meet. Unitarianism under
Emersonian stimulus met it for a time; when that
stimulus withdrew, it was enfeebled by its own breadth.
In July a man may sleep delightfully with his light tent
open to all the winds of heaven; he is rash or doomed
who repeats the fond experiment in December.

Religions begin by concentration and particularity,
by concentrating regard on particular objects, acts,
men, deities. Liberalism arrives to broaden the field of
sanctities; religion, finally, sees and uses good everywhere, in ancient foreign cult and in newborn scientific
theory, in the instinct of a child and in the profundities
of intuition. But hospitality, the sanest of virtues, may
end by turning the house into a thoroughfare — in
which case the essence of religion is lost for host and
guest alike. God, we are told (even by our Quaker
Whittiers) is contemporaneous, and the temptation
supervenes to look for him between the covers of the
latest periodical. The professors of liberal religion in
our day are nothing better than *shoppers* in contemporary literature and philosophy — shoppers who do not
buy.[1] New tokens, new embodiments, of God may
breed in a faith a hunger for novelty which, in the
dearth of other resources, may find satisfaction at last
in the consumption of its own tissue.

When religion is everywhere, it is nowhere in particular, and the people for whom maples are burning

[1] An exception to this rule is the band of so-called Unitarian Human-
ists who flourish under the courageous leadership of John H. Dietrich of
Minneapolis.

bushes are rarely found upon their knees before maples. I say rarely, because Emersons are born and reared on this irreverent or superstitious planet. They are few, and their influence cannot always halt the movements of the age toward secularity and paganism. In such ages the effect of making religion coextensive with secularity is to make secularity coessential with religion. Emerson's fate was to encounter such an age, and he is for the moment all but forgotten in the walks of his disciples. They are now insensible to his fervor, and they practice his liberality to no purpose.

IV

So much for Emerson and the present-day liberal. Has he fared better at the hands of orthodox believers? Sixty years ago Emerson and liberal religion, though not quite together, were alike in their distance from slow-pacing orthodoxy. In the time interval, the tortoise has almost overtaken the hare, but curiously enough, without the smallest profit either to Emerson or to liberal religion. In a latter-day gospel by Harry *Emerson* Fosdick called *Christianity and Progress* I could not find a single reference to Emerson. Theism in its straits might turn for aid in his direction, but it dreads that lifeboat more than the filling ship. It is actually probable that today Emerson's mere name is known to fewer Congregationalists and Presbyterians than sixty years ago. At that time the writer almost outshone the heretic, and Emerson on the arm of Longfellow and Hawthorne found access to many hearths which he could never have approached on the arm of Channing or of Parker. That chaperonage is scarcely now available, and national pride no longer fosters the kind of interest which, to take a nearer example, the undevout and unpatriotic Ibsen evokes in the patriotic and devout Norwegian.

There remains a third and still more interesting question. What is Emerson's footing with the independent nonsectarian religious thinker? James Harvey Robinson's "Religion" in *Whither Mankind?* (1928) mentions Emerson just once, casually, in a review of names. Shall we dismiss Mr. Robinson as a cold philosopher? What, then, does the man of whom Matthew Arnold wrote "A voice oracular hath peal'd today" signify to reverent and elevated spirits of our time, such as Maurice Maeterlinck and George Santayana? Maeterlinck, in a twenty-two page early essay in which the name of Emerson occurs just five times, abounds in a lyric eloquence which the reader rather inhales than digests. At the end he has told us little, has made us feel that he valued the Emersonian method more than its results, that, in short, he preferred the observatory to the firmament. The high-souled Santayana is cool, is niggardly, to Emerson. He begins a brief article with emphasis on what we may call the high emanations from the person of the seer. The emanations, of course, not being transferable to print, are not transferable to posterity, and exempt posterity, to that extent, from the necessity of veneration. He has some admirable criticism of Emerson's logic (why did he not add some criticism of Emerson's eyebrows?) and seems finally to dismiss the seer as a sublime aberration. Aberrations are least forgivable when they presume to put on sublimity.

Mr. Paul Elmer More and Dr. Irving Babbitt are distinguished among the literary critics of our time by a rare constancy — implying, in their case, a rare fortitude — in the preaching of a high and grave morality. Toward Emerson Dr. Babbitt is not unkind and Mr. More is not uncordial; but both look upon him, as it were, "with one auspicious and one drooping eye," classing him, like Santayana, as a divine prodigal to whom one brings a sparing and a wary veneration. Mr. More makes Emerson's "facile optimism" responsible for Christian Science. He also makes Arnold's "disinterested endeavor" responsible in part, through Walter Pater, for the debasement of Oscar Wilde. Perhaps the second genealogy may serve as scholium to the first.

v

Everywhere the signs seem inauspicious, but these signs do not exhaust the horoscope. The neglect into which Emerson has fallen is of another quality than the Lethe in which other saintly and prophetic leaders are immersed. Wise men to whom he is temporarily useless suspect that Emerson and the world have not cast their final reckoning together. He is the book that is not so much put up as put down — the suspended task to which in leisurely and thoughtful hours return is possible. We do not yet dare to say whether it is yesterday or tomorrow that sleeps beneath the block of unhewn quartz in Concord. The force of Emerson's life and gospel remains unexhausted, since the world did not stop to hear his preaching to the end, and the force of the human instinct to which that preaching appealed is unexpended and is inexhaustible. Both are patient, and the future is extensive. Who shall say that they will not rejoin each other?

The rendezvous may be distant; the logical interval, the logical barrier, between ourselves and Emerson is not to be lightly overleapt. But the fitting comment on Emerson's want of logic is Lincoln's on the alleged drunkenness of Grant ("Send his whisky to the other generals"). Sobriety is admirable, but one prefers — Appomattox. One could wish that Emerson had been logical — and that logicians had led equally happy and elevated lives. When Emerson has said his utmost, the logical difficulties remain; but when logic has said its utmost, Emerson remains: and Emerson is the larger remainder of the two. After all, intelligence does not subvert religion; the besiegers never win until the garrison is treacherous. The case of present-day science against religion is hardly stronger than the prescientific case of logic against Christianity, and if religion was capable of age-long survival under the second, a believer might contend that it was capable of revival under the first. The world, which loves and hates religion by turns, in and after Emerson's day had had a surfeit of religion; and its respect for logic was merely the politic veil of its reviving appetite for worldliness and pagan secularity. That movement will run its course; its decline is no less certain than its advent: mankind may return to Emerson, like Peer Gynt after his vain wanderings to the irremovable and unimpatient Solveig.

VI

In the Emersonian philosophy the instinct for fact or reason finds three chief stumblingblocks: the obedience to instinct, the favorable view of life, and the infinitude and immanence of deity. The first of these is really unimportant. When Emerson says, "Follow your instincts," the indiscretion, the audacity, is merely phrasal; and the whole context is a gloss and emendation for that phrase. "Trust thyself: every heart vibrates to that iron string." The "iron" is conclusive. We are to follow our instincts (the higher instincts) through pain and difficulty. Self-indulgence can find no harborage for its cushion or its goblet here. The Emersonian phrase may be incautious, but I doubt if in the Emersonian text it ever served as spur or cloak to license. Carve *Fay ce que vouldras* over the arched portal of a minster, and the inscription would corrupt the mind of nobody. Epicures, passing in the street, do not glance upward.

Emerson's optimism is exasperating to our pessi-

mism, but we must remember that Emerson's knowledge of evil would almost have qualified another man
for pessimism, and that the ground for pessimism itself is scarcely either logical or scientific. It is curious
that Emerson's psychic altitude never suggests to the
critics at what we may call sea level what physical
altitude so instantly and powerfully suggests — the possibility of a wider and clearer outlook. Drenched with
rain, you cannot repress your anger at the man who
proclaims that the sky is all sunshine and azure; it
never occurs to you that his standing-ground may be
above the clouds.

The question of theism offers undoubtedly a more
serious problem. Discussion within my limits is impossible, but it may be noted that the theistic ideal
underwent in Emerson's hands a harder test than any
to which science or logic could subject it — the ordeal
of lifelong experiment. William James in *The Varieties
of Religious Experience* declares that Emerson never
makes it quite clear whether his God is an *order* or a
being, whether it should be called infinite benevolence
or, simply, infinite benefit. If this were true, one side
of this double possibility would span more than half
the interval between Emerson and current thought.
Science, moreover, has been successively both theistic
and non-theistic (i.e., agnostic), and, if it now leans
away from Emerson, we must remember that, in relation to time, space, and matter, it has lately added to
its other demonstrated powers a noticeable power of

self-reversal. When science locks a door in the face of protesting orthodoxy or theism, the place in which it drops the key is not the cistern but its own pocket.

<h2 style="text-align:center">VII</h2>

The last thing to be said is that Emerson is not a notion; he is a *fact*. Emerson is history; he is there in the unchanging record, as indelible as Runnymede, as inexpugnable as Gibraltar. Let us restate in a single terse word his originality: to put (in practice as in theory) the whole weight and worth of the universe at its best behind each object and behind each moment of experience. The premise may be real or illusory. If real, the signal fact in the history of our race has been its capacity in one man to appropriate this reality. If illusory, one is still half moved to say that the signal fact in the history of our race has been its power to originate this illusion. Illusion or reality, it represents the highest *yield* of life.

Most persons now feel that the facts are against Emerson. But science itself in our day is oddly busy at the task of removing the virility, the old-time pugnacity, from the word "fact." Fact is the reflection of the object in the subject; blur the object, blur the subject, approximate or knead together object and subject, and fact, like atom, tends swiftly to lose its granular and contumacious quality. Knowledge becomes an occasion for experience, an inlet to experience, and its virtue is not the virtue of a transcript but an application. But

it is just here that the hope in Emerson, the hope for
Emerson, revives. Emerson means for us pre-eminently
an enlargement of the possibilities of man's experience;
the inextinguishable thirst of the race for what is larger
and deeper in the psychic life cannot finally ignore him.
He has achieved the unforeseen, the unimagined; the
impossible is humbled in his presence; and the race will
come back to him as the supplanted heir comes back to
search in a neglected cabinet for the lost title deed to a
disputed fortune.

THE LAST OF THE MOUNTAINEERS

THE letters of William Dean Howells have been given to the public and the moment seems ripe for a glance at the relation between Howells and our own contemporaries, or rather at the relation between his work and theirs. The two relations are far from being one. If Howells had died in 1900, we should have exclaimed in 1920: "What would he say of us today?" But Howells did live till 1920, and said nothing vitriolic. He felt differences singularly little, and his juniors felt that little was to be gained by emphasizing their differences from Howells. Moreover, the movement in fiction which he headed prevailed until his death, prevails today. Fiction is still, in aim and matter, largely realistic, and it still seeks in art and style that *look* of spontaneity which Howells praised in style and not only praised but realized in art. The practice was much safer for him than for his juniors, because the dullard cannot distinguish the look of spontaneity from the fact, and the *fact* of spontaneity is — for the dullard — the negation of all that is valuable in art and style. It remains true, however, that in the crusade which Howells undertook in the eighties he has practically triumphed. The only trouble is that, when you are actually in Jerusalem, you begin to wonder if the Christians, after all, are so much better than the Turks. That happens after Godfrey of Bouillon is dead.

The difference in spirit between Howells and our time is real, and, to understand it, we must look back toward that efflorescence of New England in the mid-nineteenth century which found in the novelist the latest of its eminent disciples. Between 1830 and 1880 New England led the country in a movement which combined worship, freedom, culture, taste, and ethics in happy harmony and just proportion. The literary worth of that movement need not be argued here. Let me say only that its poetry, except in flashes, was not superlative, that it produced four, if not five, strong prose styles, that it produced a great novelist, a *causeur* worthy of Paris, and in Emerson an occurrence — I use the word advisedly — the momentousness of which is still unguessed by an insouciant posterity. But my immediate point is not literary, but human. In that day man as man stood high; as man he has since undoubtedly declined. To the mixture of reverences and affections just noted I shall for the moment give the name humanity; and to that mixture Howells, geographically an Ohioan, fell heir. A very few words will now make clear his relation both to the elder and to the later time.

In 1850 humanity in New England produced romance — *The Scarlet Letter*. In 1879 fiction, having added realism to humanity, produced *The Lady of the Aroostook*. In 1920 fiction, having kept realism and dropped humanity, produced *Main Street*. In Howells the two movements, the elder in its vigorous recession and the younger in its strong maturity, came together; and the combination made Howells. Howells answers a question: "What happens to realism when character, sympathy, reverence, and taste are added to the realist?" *Main Street* also answers a question: "What happens to realism when character, sympathy, reverence, and taste are excluded, not from the realist's life of course, but from his workshop?" The new realism wants to draw the *bare* man as seen by the *naked* eye. But there is no naked eye; an eye is a mass of sheaths and coverlets. So is a man even with his clothes off. Criteria, judgments, cannot be excluded. *Main Street* itself is a verdict, a verdict of "Guilty" against unintelligence and unprogressiveness. But if verdicts on intelligence and progressiveness are lawful, why not verdicts on morality and taste? The human race is like Peer Gynt's onion; our wrappages are all there is of us.

The truth is that the more a man is, the more he understands. Every gain to being is an aid to comprehension. All restraining forces like conscience and taste understand both themselves and their opposites; the opposites can understand nothing but themselves. Strangely enough, delicacy can draw either delicacy or coarseness better than coarseness can. It would be unfair to ask Mr. Dreiser to draw a Bromfield Corey, but ought he not to draw a Frank Cowperwood better than Howells? Frank Cowperwood is not ill drawn, but compare him with Bartley Hubbard, a character of the same predacious type, and he does not merely sink into offal; he vanishes into smoke. Howells' revolt from Bartley, since it is a seeing and not a blind revolt, is a powerful esthetic re-enforcement. Sherwood Anderson, vibrant in distemper, is a temperament, making forays and seeking pasturage in other temperaments. What should he know of character? I should have rejoiced to see a delineation of Sherwood Anderson by Howells, but I would not turn a corner or turn a page to find a delineation of Howells by Sherwood Anderson.

Taste and conscience are not hindrances, but helps. They are biases, to be sure, but everything positive enough to be useful is a bias; a nervous system is a bias. Expectation governs eyesight; we see only the fulfillment or the contravention of our expectations. The more we feel, the more ways we feel, the more kinds of expectations we have, the wider and richer is the esthetic outlook. Every principle is a boundary, a Danube or Rio Grande, on the opposing sides of which contending tribesmen face each other in exciting contrast. It is a singular and most suggestive fact that even a frivolous principle like etiquette is made in *The Rise of Silas Lapham* the groundwork of the most enlivening appeals. A new criterion is like a new sense; it enlarges and diversifies the object. All this is true, and doubly and emphatically true, of ethical distinctions.

The ancient morality with its religious sanction shed a beam from the Great White Throne or a shadow from Gehenna on a dozen humble alternatives in the progress of a workman's simple day. Such a concept may be ignorant, may be chimerical, but its esthetic power is undeniable and plain. Even granting that a second esthetic exists which denies and excludes the first, that would no more prove that the first was unreal than a war between the Welsh and the Cornishmen would prove that the Welsh — or the Cornish either — were not Cymry. The place for the twentieth-century vagary that makes morality a bugaboo to art is on the same ash heap with the seventeenth-century chimera that made art a hobgoblin to morality. Away with the finical and ignominious notion that the faculties which house together in the same brain are foes or strangers, like the common occupants of a New York apartment house, who do not speak in the elevator. Man is not a squabble but a league, and his parts are not anchorites but co-workers. Nature, the ultimate realist, has no scruples about the approximation of use and beauty. Curiously enough, the favorite topic of artists of this school is sex, and sex, that is, esthetic rapture on a ground of biological necessity, is Nature's original and definitive repudiation of their creed.

Howells, then, brought to the examination of life the full equipment of a highly civilized and astonishingly gifted man. Our own realism, on the contrary, wants to simplify, to strip, and to despoil the man before it sends him out to discover what his fellow men are like. Howells possessed the perennial source and spring of all sound realism, a love and respect for the object of its study. Realism without affection for reality is an atheist saying Mass. Too much — not all — of our fiction doubts or even denies the value of the life and persons whom it draws. When John How-ells, the novelist's son, said at thirty-one that he didn't know what life was for, the father remarked: "I was fifty before I didn't know what it was for." Wasn't it object enough to be W. D. H.'s son or J. M. H.'s father? Question, denial, meet us everywhere. Mr. Dreiser un-covers our venalities and carnalities to the admiration of Mr. Mencken; Mr. Masters publishes a remarkable satire that is more devastating than Juvenal without being — and this completes and clinches the indict-ment — half so earnest; and across the ocean the most popular biography of our time devotes itself to the melancholy task of suggesting that a good woman may be contemptible. Is this the climate for realism? An age like ours should be writing *Vatheks* and *Undines;* by all the congruities and coherencies of things despair should find its mandragora in romance; Mr. Cabell's far from charmless *Domnei* is more to the purpose than Herrick's *Waste.* Observation tends to become either contemptuous, prophylactic (the mouse's observation of the cat), or, it may be, simply mechanical, as if a criminal on the scaffold should count the buttons on the headman's coat.

Are we tired of realism without daring or caring to

admit the fact? Do we begin to seek escape or, at worst, distraction? Strange prowlers like expressionism are heard in the sullen outskirts of our drama. In fiction Mr. Wilder goes to Peru to discuss theology (if I wanted to discuss theology, I *would* go to Peru). Mr. O'Neill, a most vivid personality, really original, inherently poetic, is incapable of the smallest interest in an undemonstrative person in a quiet situation, and has to seek respites from the irksomeness of actuality by sorties into the monstrous. The great resource, the chance which perhaps accounts for the preservation of realism in titular ascendency until this hour, has been the opening up of new territory in the unpathed wilderness of sex. Realism plunged into the wild with the relief — the temporary or temporizing relief — with which land-seekers rush into an opened reservation. Here was material at once actual and new; here was virgin realism, virgin, I had almost said, to the ravisher. The barriers of the tenable doctrine, the treatable situation, and the printable word were moved forward with a strange speed and a portentous unanimity. So far as speech goes, I have no quarrel with the removal of the landmarks of decency to a more rational and less confining distance; what I deplore is that in the feast which celebrated this removal Priapus should have headed the procession. It is curious, again, that there should be so little blitheness in our animality. Our voluptuousness has a belated, elderly, unquiet air, as a man of sixty-five who, after long sobrieties, feeling that he has missed life, installs a chorus girl in an apartment.

I say too much. There is another side. Miss Ruth Suckow is a perfectly sincere and highly sympathetic realist; she has an art that Howells would have stroked. Faithful observers whom he did stroke remain among us; Mr. Tarkington faces life with amused nonchalance, Mr. Garland with reproachful candor. Mr. Hergesheimer has a lazy, muscular force, as of a mastiff sleeping in a courtyard. Mrs. Wharton, marvelously endowed, gives to actuality itself the effect of a superb exotic; in Mrs. Gerould a bitter insight finds solace in resentful scintillations. Our poetry as a whole is not despicable; it has much novel ingenuity and some real feeling. In a drama which seems crumbling all about us, Mr. O'Neill, if not yet, not demonstrably, a great force, is a great figure.

These things should be duly weighed. No weight that we may care to give them, however, will alter the fact that a new Howells in our day would be almost inconceivable, and the reason is instructive to the last degree. A man of his talents could be born tomorrow quite as imaginably as in 1837; what we can scarcely suppose is that a character like his could be born, or, if born, could be reared, in our surroundings. Nor is it clear that we are rearing other types of equal value. It is odd that our perfect willingness to follow Madame Bovary into every winding of her psychology and physiology has turned so few of us into Flauberts. Even the Flauberts, it would seem, have other origins. Release of the primitive has proved less profitable than we expected. Each of us felt that he caged within himself a wild animal which, if uncaged, would make his fortune in the gaping street. But, unluckily for the desired sensation, the strong wild things had died of heat and of confinement. The Hairy Ape in the O'Neill cage was the unique exception.

The disease of our literature is the disease of civilization itself; where life has no standard, letters can have none. When the house is on fire, to save the library you must save the house. I propose to speak briefly of the house, of life in general. We lack character and principle, the seeds no less of a sound life than of a generous realism. Because we lack them, we order our lives at the bidding or suggestion of forces like science with its offshoot evolution or progress with its servant internationalism. All these are, or have been, ameliorative forces, but they should have no control of our purposes and standards, and, in the unlicensed exercise of that control, they have all but remanded us to our primitive instincts. Our sole help lies in the establishment within ourselves of a principle that can judge these forces and resist them where resistance is desirable. In a word, not one of them should influence our ends.

Those ends should be fixed by the race's deliberate estimate of what is most to be admired and sought in human character. Men agree more than they suppose they agree on the overwhelmingly decisive point of human excellence. They are agreed on Isaiah, on Socrates and Epictetus, on Regulus and Winkelried, on Angelo, on Pascal, on Alfred the Great, on Thomas More and Thomas Browne, on Lessing, on Emerson, on Lincoln, on Cardinal Mercier; they tend to agreement on Shelley. From such unanimities one might almost deduce a recipe or formula for man. I hinted at such a formula when I suggested that the New England movement, which found a mellow epilogue in Howells, combined worship, freedom, culture, taste, and ethics. It is clear that the difficult ingredient is worship. The other requirements are at least within the grasp of aspiration, but the passage of the old theology and of much — if not most — of the old theism has left us without guidance and without obvious resource in this particular. Intellectually, Howells himself dwelt only in the religious afterglow, but his character was shaped by its meridian.

Christianity was in fact a revelation, but not of God; what it revealed was man. It shed light on human possibilities. The variety in its forms was large; the variety in its disciples was immense: these two facts made it an experiment on a secular and mundane scale in the reaction of the heart of man to stimuli. Here and there, with the right helps, it produced extraordinary beings. It could not do this long or often or unaided; this indeed was rarely what it tried to do. Columbus, sailing for India, stumbled on America; Christianity, fumbling for deity, discovered man. The point is to respect and preserve its success in acknowledging its failure. Almost nobody is sane enough to grasp the double fact that Christianity is a sinking ship with treasure in its hold. That treasure is the veneration of its best disciples for life and for man. Everybody acts, it would seem, on the highly uncommercial supposition that the cargo of a sinking ship cannot be valuable. Mr. Julian Huxley in his "Religion without Revelation" sees at least that there is something to be saved; only I fear that the boat to which he transfers the treasure is a cockleshell. The faith which bred the veneration for life and man is irrecoverable; the future of the race may hinge on the question whether, being irrecoverable, it is also irreplaceable — whether, in a word, its benefits are irrecoverable. I find it hard to think that a permanently valuable state of mind can have for its one possible source an intrinsically evanescent fable. That something like the type we want can be produced outside of Christianity is proved, I think, by the Greek Sophocles.

Science should be viewed as an irrelevance. Our age in its spiritual penury need not fear the tolls of science for the same reason that the beggar does not dread the tax collector. Indeed, we are released from real embarrassments. We are free from the burden of reconciling nature and virtue, a burden cast upon us by the old belief that the sources of nature and virtue were identical. Moreover, the absence of any known supreme intelligence clears the ground in a fashion for man. There is no proved superior mind to urge its purposes upon him, or divert him from the pursuit of the best that experiment has uncovered in his own nature. He is left master at least of his hopes, his standards, and his wishes. Science, lastly, is an arsenal of means; the chooser of ends can afford to disregard it.

There remains the superstition of progress. Not all progress need be classed as superstition. Progress in knowledge, progress in invention, may be real, since a store may be indefinitely greatened. Anglo-Saxons have progressed in liberty. But in the artistic, ethical, and kindred fields, though advance is possible, oscillation is more feasible than advance. These oscillations are exposed to criticism like other movements, and they evade that criticism by taking to themselves the name, the authority, and the seductiveness of progress. A man may progress toward Tyburn; a man need only turn upon his heel for recession to become progress; and it is not without interest that the most widely acclaimed poem of the last forty years should have borne the strange title of "Recessional." The truth is that a state or an age, like a man, may have inducements to do good or ill, and the juggle of progress in that case is to turn the temptation into a precept — in other words, to make a sheriff of the footpad. The reasons for the present vogue of progress are partly the great momentum and the strong cohesion of the age, and partly the want of any inward permanent sense of what men

can and ought to be. In this uncertainty proffers take
the aspect of demands; not knowing what we want, we
buy what the salesman progress undertakes to sell us.
In literature and art we turn from whim to later whim,
like a countryman in an art museum, passing from one
object to the next, not because he wants to see that
object, but because it is the next. Of internationalism
a word only can be said. We move helplessly in the
direction of a world-wide mixture of the traits of all
nationalities, though there is not the slightest reason to
believe that such a mixture would be half as good as
France or England or even couchant Italy or humbled
Germany today.

All these forces may be good. Their ascendency is
the evil; they help where they do not govern. They
have drifted into the place left vacant by the abdication
of the human spirit in the bewilderment following the
inevitable passage of its ancient guide and counselor,
inherited Christianity. That human spirit should resume its sway. All vain and fantastic theories to the
contrary notwithstanding, the redemption of literature,
its enfranchisement and prosperity, lie in its participation in a movement for the redemption of the spirit of
man as a whole from its ignoble bondage. Art is the
child of life, and, being its child, should be its sustenance and stay; filial piety is among the few remaining virtues which our listlessly ironic age consents to
honor. The time will come when men will look back
with scorn and amazement at the pitiful criticism

which ignores material, which emphasizes virtuosity, which finds its criterion in the agreement of the result with the intention, a procedure manifestly inept since one of the two elements to be compared is inaccessible to observation. Subject and aim, their quality and grade, are all-important. The man who, like Howells, paints the good in men's lives that it may be loved and the ill in men's lives that it may be mended, being the real human being, is the true artist.

I have called Howells the last of the mountaineers, the last eminent survivor of a generous and high tradition. That tradition even yet survives in a way, but it survives like a fleet after a hurricane — in parted fragments. Once worship, freedom, culture, taste, and ethics coexisted. Today worship persists among the uncultivated; culture survives among the irreligious. Among the cultivated, morality is shamefaced and freedom tongue-tied. These parted seafarers have no rendezvous. The question is if they, by chance or effort, can rejoin each other. That reunion is the object of our quest. Changing our figure, yet still keeping a glimpse of sea-blue in the distance, we are now in the condition of the Greeks in Xenophon's *Anabasis* after the fall of their ambitious leader, the young Cyrus. We have been tempted far from home and country; we find ourselves in the heart of a barbaric empire with strange complexions, curious usages, and alien garb. Nothing remains to us but the long and arduous return, the grim journey in which arrival is doubtful, but privation sure. We may faint in the long labor of the march; we may drop our brittle lives in the swollen river, on the icy peak, or in the blinding sand. Fainting or failing, we must still push on. The cry of "Θάλασσα! Θάλασσα!" may come at last to end and to requite our toil; but, if we fall before we hear or raise that shout, we may die at least with foot and eye turned westward, with heart and breath forward reaching, in latest throb and parting sigh, toward Hellas and the sea.

THE IRRESPONSIBLE POWER
OF REALISM

⇶⇶⇶⇶⇶⇶⇶⇶⇶⇶⇶⇶⇶》《⇇⇇⇇⇇⇇⇇⇇⇇⇇⇇⇇

Ours is an age that sifts the qualifications of teachers. Realistic fiction is one of its most powerful and popular teachers, yet realistic fiction is never asked to demonstrate its right to teach. It passes no test; it produces no credentials. The case has indeed some manifest peculiarities. Realistic fiction does not profess to teach; it merely teaches. The realistic reader does not register for the school; he merely learns. Obviously, however, if a professed fiction is believed to be true and is not true, the harm, though not the guilt, is as great as if the deception were intentional.

All this came about in a most innocent and guileless way. Fiction, striving mainly for amusement, found that parts of truth were amusing; insensibly, as time went on, it increased both the truth and the stress upon the truth. But there were no claims and no securities. The writer told as much truth as he could or as he chose; the reader believed as little or as much as he could or as he chose. Meanwhile, in every other field, the age showed an increasing rigor in its demands on teachers and its tests of truth; it would have seemed that in such an age the survival in one quarter of a mixed body of truth and falsehood exciting in the reader's mind a mixture of belief and doubt was impossible. The pressure of science should logically have given birth to one of two results: the expulsion of error from the books, or the eradication of belief from the reader. Fiction met neither of these demands, yet its power, particularly its power as teacher, steadily increased. It holds now, among other truth tellers, the post of an unofficial informant, an unacknowledged counselor, a Colonel House, as it were, whose undertone, in President Wilson's ear, was as powerful as the voice of cabinets or embassies. It is a power that may err, and for its errors there is usually no remedy (confutation is only now and then effectual), and almost always no punishment. In a word, its power is irresponsible.

Let us survey for a moment the justice and propriety of this arrangement, and later review some of the conditions which make this power weighty and dangerous in our own time.

I

Realistic fiction, for our purposes, is a wide term, including all fiction, prosaic and poetical, dramatic and narrative, which makes any serious attempt at accuracy in the delineation of life. The reader's views of life and man, of the worth of both, may be materially affected by the pictures and the estimates, express or tacit, of life and humanity to be found in its pages. The first observation to be made is that a very strong case, though a case somewhat stronger in form than in substance, could be made out for the total exclusion of fiction of any kind from the court in which these weighty issues are debated. Realistic fiction is a combination of truth and falsehood with no frontier between the true and the false; no proof is offered of any affirmation, and, in strictness, nothing is affirmed — no sentence is declared by its author to be true. Indeed, so curious is the blend of seriousness and frivolity in the mind of the novel-reading public that if an author printed in red ink or italicized or starred (as Louisa Mühlbach, the historical novelist, is said to have done) every sentence that he knew or thought to be true, a proceeding so agreeable to honesty and common sense would be visited with pitiless derision.

As matters now stand, no court would give an instant's hearing to the account of a real murder in a novel, though the novelist were Tolstoy, yet the race will accept precisely similar testimony in a process which concerns, not indeed its life or death, but its justifications for living or dying. The anomaly becomes clear if we imagine a demand for credit on the part of a like mixture of truth and fable in science. The mixture of voluntary lie with truth in a page of a textbook in physics is unthinkable; indeed the mixture of involuntary error with truth in the proportion of one to five hundred is enough to doom the book and shame the author. A final question may be put. Why should a man who is alive, with all the immensity of personal resource inhering in those two momentous syllables, take life at second hand from authors who do not trouble themselves to assert, much less to prove, the verity of their own pictures?

The plea is cogent, cogent almost to excess. Of the clumsiness of fiction as a carrier of truth there can be no doubt. In an ideal world verisimilitude in fiction would be viewed as a help to art, not as a path to knowledge. Nevertheless, we are faced by a condition, not a theory. In the actual world fiction *does* contain truth; it *does* create belief; it *does* implant convictions. It even molds history. *Uncle Tom's Cabin* buttressed the Emancipation Proclamation. If fiction ceased to inform, what other informant would take its place? History and biography? Excellent as these are, in sifting the truths from the falsehoods, they leave half the interest in the dustbin; fiction sifts a treasure from the rubbish. The best biography extant — Boswell's *Life of Johnson* — is the biography whose method approaches closest to that of the novel. If history will not serve, shall we resort to experience, to life itself, for information? Emphatically, yes; yet if our lives are in one sense *lived novels,* they are novels which it is impossible for most of us to write and difficult for many of us to read. Life, so vast and so near, eludes us by its nearness and its vastness. "It's a puzzlin' world," said Mr. Tulliver; and philosophy must grimly acquiesce. Fiction tries at least to solve the puzzle. It offers a picture with a picture's oneness; it presents a view with a view's solidarity. It is, in a word, receivable, consumable, and is accepted by many minds in lieu of life itself for precisely the same reason that a wheat-raiser, seeking food, would prefer his grocer's inferior flour to his own superior wheat, provided that his wheat were unground. Again, if meal and bran are mixed in fiction, there are sieves of a kind in the reader's own establishment. He has not lived a quarter or a half century quite in vain. He knows certain things to be true; he finds the *verum* sometimes, the *verisimile* rather often. Truth has its own savor, like vanilla or pineapple, which the trained palate recognizes, more or less distinctly, in the artistic combinations of which it forms a part.

Such is the apology for the qualified acceptance of the very peculiar testimony offered by realistic fiction as to the nature, conduct, and lot of man. We speak only of its function as a carrier of knowledge; of its worth as entertainment and as art there should be no question in our time. It should be said, further, in its defense, that the position of its authors is, in form at least, impregnable. Their attitude might equally well be the perfection of modesty or the perfection of strategy; in point of fact, it is probably neither the one nor the other, but the unforeseen, and more or less unconscious, growth of circumstance. Furnishing truth with falsehood, they ask no credence even for their truth. They label the entire compound fiction. In the end perhaps they may come to resemble a manufacturer who should put large quantities of butter into his oleomargarine, should dutifully label the mixture with the less reputable name, and should finally profit by the impression spreading in the neighborhood that the percentage of butter in the compound was greater than it actually was. The credence the fiction writers get is, historically, not a theft, but a gift, from the public. None the less, it is an irresponsible power, and it behooves us to look a little narrowly at the novel conditions which make its exercise at the present hour particularly significant and momentous.

II

Realistic fiction observes; it is part of that general observation and experiment of life which in the last century or so has come to be the only authoritative spokesman on destiny and man. The case was once quite different. A century ago men's ideas on these subjects — often very clear and sure ideas — were drawn, not from inductions, not from a man's own eyes and ears and heart and mind nor from the tongues and pens of conscientious fellow witnesses, but from an ancient, sacred, and unerring book. Why go to *Hamlet* or to the *Canterbury Tales* to find out what you were taught in Genesis? Evidence was worthless in the face of knowledge. The best of ascertainable facts brought no solace, as the worst of ascertainable facts brought no dismay, to a mind prepossessed with the conviction that human nature was essentially depraved. If this was true of discovered facts, it was more emphatically true of invented fictions. Iago was a bad man, but a theology which saw Iagos everywhere, even in Othellos and Desdemonas, was not likely to find in the most lifelike Iago that inspiration could produce a ground for the revisal of its estimate of human nature.

Of course depravity was not the entire story; a divine power dwelt at the heart of things in whose mercies predestined individuals were to share. But this, again, was only pre-established certainty in the more attractive form of pre-established guarantee. With sanctity installed in the core of things, what need to investigate the surface — except indeed for the incidentally useful objects of inhabiting and traversing the surface? The virtue that observation could detect became irrelevant, if not positively misleading. With deity as reservoir, the supply, in so far as the supply could be tapped, was inexhaustible; with the Mississippi practically domesticated in one's bathroom, why calculate the standing water in the pipes? Fiction, like history, might still be useful; it might portray, divert, inform, impel: but the final word as to the value of man's life and nature belonged to other and more august voices.

When this theology was shaken in the mid-nineteenth century, a main agent in its overthrow was the theory of evolution, and, oddly enough, this very doctrine became the source of another form of pre-established guarantee. Men did not turn to life and man and ask frankly: "What are you worth?" On the contrary, they proceeded to deduce these values from a generalization vaster and more comprehensive than that which had dispensed Augustine and Calvin from the necessity of examining the facts. It seemed incredible that man and man's life should not be valuable when they were parts of a system that turned savages into Platos and apes into men, though the fact that so few savages became Platos and so few species rose into men argued a certain unevenness and partiality in the distribution of the bounties of the universe. It seemed to the more hopeful spirits that religion, forsaking its harshness, and science, renouncing its austerity, smiled together on a world predestined to unspeakable fruitions. The world's state was convalescence, and the ills which fact or realistic fiction might report were viewed as lightly as the restrictions and sufferings that meet one in the cheerful reascent to health. Then came the disquiet and querulousness of the closing nineteenth century; then, in 1914, the World War. The virility of optimism was broken. Civilization was saved — at last — perhaps; but it was hard to believe that the evolution which had permitted its agony would have recoiled from its death. That strange power had done, might still do, miracles of beneficence, but we had no longer the heart to affirm that we as individuals, our nation, our race, or even our planet, were its protégés.

The consequence of all this was, in one way, very simple. The evolutionary presumption had followed the theological presumption into limbo; the era of presumptions was over; the way was cleared for the examination of facts. Now inspection or induction had been from the first the primary and natural method of ascertaining these transcendent values; it had been kept in abeyance through the preoccupation of the ground by secondary and artificial methods. Nothing more had taken place than what happens every night in our theaters when the wrongful occupant of a seat is displaced, and the owner takes the chair to which he is entitled. But, in another sense, the situation brought about by this displacement was critical, almost tragical, in its implications. The weight of significance that was now thrown upon what simple inspection at first or second hand could tell us about life was fearful to contemplate. The race might approach such an ordeal with feelings akin to those of the man in *The Suicide Club* turning up the card which might or might not be the death-bringing ace of spades. Yesterday inspection had been relatively unimportant because the case had been vouched for by evolution or theology. A man holding a promissory note given by an unknown and suspected debtor, but guaranteed by a world-famed capitalist, learns suddenly that the indorser's signature is a forgery. The question of the solvency and integrity of the first signer, which was yesterday a secondary matter, rises at a bound to a position of superlative importance.

Realistic fiction, as has already been intimated, is only one of the elements that bear the weight of this increased responsibility; it is not even foremost on the list. Every conscious moment is an observation or experiment in life, and the value of the aggregate of these inductions is enormous. There is also the testimony of our fellows embodied in history, biography, and the other forms of the literature of fact. Realistic fiction is a secondary, but very significant, partner in the great investigation, and when we compare the lightness of its original purpose with the gravity of the causes in which its evidence is required, we feel as if a ballet dancer had been called into court to give weighty testimony as to an archbishop's honor.

III

To this last comparison the prompt and fair retort would be, Why not? If a ballet dancer knew anything material about a prosecuted archbishop, the most austere of judges would call her into court. If fiction knows anything about life, let its voice be heard by all means in the court where life is on trial. In both cases, however, the veracity of the witness would be rigorously sifted, and the rigor would be increased if the testimony were at once adverse and crushing. Now, for a century or more, the testimony of realistic artists about life has been, on the whole, decidedly unfavorable. It becomes in our day increasingly unfavorable. We do not here quarrel with this judgment. We are not pronouncing, or reviewing, a decision; we are testing the credibility of a witness. Realistic fiction is a craft like other crafts. Does it help men to think justly about life? Does it help men to say about life just what they really think? If a jury of fifty were appointed to sit on the value of human nature and destiny, should we care to have literary artists represented in force upon that jury? How does it happen that the sternness and gloom which permeate realism are rarely or never found in men whose business is the investigation of human nature and conduct by other and severer methods, in publicists, economists, statisticians, historians, biographers? In trying to answer these questions, we shall bear in mind that the business of realistic fiction is not to judge life but to draw it. This is true beyond a doubt, true in exactly the same sense that it is the business of a druggist to sell drugs and not cigars. Realistic artists do not profess judgment; they merely practice it, as *Anna Karenina, Tess of the D' Urbervilles, Strife, The Weavers, Widowers' Houses,* and *Main Street* clearly prove. In a sense, they practice wthout a license, since their opinions commonly win a respect proportioned to their artistic, not their judicial, competence.

Artists are rarely judges; they feel but do not weigh. Their relation to the world is exceptional; their demands are exigent and peculiar. The artist is sometimes an Athenian in Bœotia; he brings the higher sensibility to a world accommodated to the lower. Sufferings actually greater than those of his fellows are greatened once more in the perspective of his imagination, and greatened a third time in the reflector of his art. As artist he is committed at the outset to a point of view which has no necessary or permanent relation to the distinction between true and false. His field is the portrayable, and he is bound by this initial bias to prefer the portrayable falsehood to the unportrayable truth, the portrayable gloom to the unportrayable sunshine. If he sternly excludes the false from his matter, it is next to impossible to bar it from his treatment. Art is the imposition upon life of a unity which life itself does not acknowledge. It is precisely in this stronghold of its unity that a generally veracious book is least trustworthy because it is least disinterested.

Let us borrow an illustration from painting. Suppose a painter put fifty animals on one canvas, all black, black mammals, black birds, black fishes, black snakes, black insects. Blackness would be the unifying principle, and the painting, even if realistic, would be worthless as testimony to the prevalence of black in the animal colorings of our globe. But let him take as his unifying principle some quality apart from color, grace of form, for example, and if, then, three-fifths or more of the animals were discovered to be black, an inference as to the frequency of black in the animal colorings of the planet would be quite legitimate. Substitute literature for painting and sadness or evil for the black colors. Plainly, if the sadness and evil belong, as they almost invariably do, to the unifying principle, if they are part of a design to depress and terrify, they no longer indicate the preference of the universe or even the artist's unbribed judgment as a human being. The darkness on the canvas no longer measures the darkness in the street or even in the studio. This may be good for art, but it falsifies evidence.

The artistic bias is commendable in an artist; it is part of his endowment. But, if he happens to be teacher or partisan, he is subject to another bias which is equally dangerous and rather less forgivable. Didactic or esthetic, the unifying principle is dictatorial; it coerces, warps, or silences the adverse facts. The allegiance of all the facts to Zola or Ibañez is preternatural — not one recreant or deserter in the host; the reader whose own facts are always defying his generalizations is amazed at this unanimous docility. The partisan novelist, like almost every other partisan, apparently believes that the inclusion of a single adverse or disquieting fact is capitulation. Philanthropy in defense of its cause is only a little less unscrupulous than motherhood in defense of its offspring. Even when authentic, the facts are brought in not as volunteers but as conscripts, and how can their true sense, their quality and meaning, declare itself under the pressure of a discipline that effaces all peculiarity in the uniformity of subjection to a militant purpose?

Either as artist or partisan, therefore, the realist is a discredited witness. There is another point in which the discredit belongs pre-eminently to the writer of our own day. The witness himself appears to be deteriorating. Once he was the offset to his own testimony. In earlier times against Dotheboys Hall we set — Dickens; against *Hard Cash* we set — Charles Reade; when George Eliot said "Tito Melema," our retort was "George Eliot." Such pictures contrasted with such painters might seem terrifying, but they also seemed anomalous, and the terror was abated by the anomaly. Even Ibsen, though less compassionate and less self-forgetful, seemed to stand like a bastion between us and his vacuous and temporizing world. But later times do not produce these consolations. Strindberg is no compensation for Miss Julia; Miss Julia and he are on the same side of the ledger. In a play like *War,* Artzibasheff manages to include himself among the objects of the reader's consternation. America is saner ground, but the images — mostly neutral — of Mr. Lewis, Mr. Dreiser, and Mr. Masters which their poems and tales suggest scarcely repair the discouragement implanted by their works. The effect of belatedness, of adhesion to an earlier school, in the sincere and generous M. Brieux is a sarcastic comment on the times. M. France, on the other hand, is personally almost an added reason for "despising man tenderly."

In our day a lighter and colder type of mind has applied itself to the delineation of anguishes and squalors which a century ago would have been left to redeemers and evangelists. Despair — at least despair on paper — is almost fashionable and attracts the type of mind which is susceptible to fashion. But the facile despairs are insignificant; the despair that really counts is that which has achieved the overthrow of large and serious and robust hopes. Hopelessness goes with want of character. The names of half a dozen virtues, industry, resolution, perseverance, patience, fortitude, courage, heroism, are nothing but the indirect affirmation of the fact that the world is penal for the trifler, the idler, and the hedonist. Hope will wane as character recedes, estimates of life will shrink as personalities diminish. The object in current literature seems to be to find out what report the world would make of itself to a mind relieved of faith, of hope, of charity, of earnestness, of distinction. Not of course that these qualities are absent from the men who write; they are absent only from their point of view as writers. One might almost as reasonably strip a man of his clothes, his shoes, his house, and his fire, in order to get from him a quite impartial judgment on the merits of life from the body's point of view. Preadjustments are imperative in both cases. The universe is brusque and shy; it shows its best side only to its best friends, and the heaviest discounts must be made from the reports of its enemies or even of the nominally impartial neutrals who have failed to gain its confidence. Let it always be remembered that we are judging of realistic fiction in its quality as witness. It is a pointed, if obvious, remark that in a court the best witness is the most intelligent and conscientious man. It would seem as if the sum of human faculty were what one should bring to the presentation of a case in which life and man are judges, plaintiffs, and defendants.

This sum of human faculty seems less and less discoverable in the realistic witnesses of our time. Sometimes the matter that wrings, or should wring, men's souls is treated as a convenience, plaything, or utensil. Or, again, men merge themselves in their themes, hardly caring to discriminate their own lives or natures from the confusion, the distress, the ignominy which they paint. Poor human vessels, heaving rudderless in a gloomy and tempestuous sea, are viewed, not from the safe and lighted shore, with its equipment of beacons and lifeboats, but from another deck, tossing helplessly in the same gloom and tempest. Mr. Dos Passos, with his rarely vivific touch, writes *Three Soldiers,* in which everybody's speech is sown with execrations, and the book itself seems like another execration.

We have mentioned some of the motives and conditions which prompt realistic fiction to the portrayal of life and man in saddening or terrifying colors. Smaller motives are allowed an equal freedom; indeed, almost any motive seems large enough to inspire that *superbe allegresse* with which, according to Jules Lemaître, the French youth of his time applied themselves to their destructive recreations. Mr. Masefield, in the narratives that succeeded *The Everlasting Mercy,* seems to have been enthralled by a species of voluptuousness in anguish. Pride in the priority of disenchantment is a second motive. There is likewise the love of a bonfire. Finally, let it not be overlooked that despair itself is merchandise, and is marketable sometimes at two dollars a copy.

IV

It is a notable fact that the new power of realistic fiction as an intepreter of life and man should have coincided with an hour of supreme crisis and calamity in the world's history, an hour when the forces that assault and the forces that protect civilization seem balanced with a nicety that defies the competence of foresight. A little thing may turn a hesitating scale; realistic fiction is not a little thing; it is entirely conceivable that in a day like ours this literary force should hold the casting vote, that its report of the worth of life and of man, adding itself to forces still more potent, might arm or disarm, might nerve or unnerve, a faltering race for victory in its final grip with anarchy and ruin. These are formidable powers; it is hard to divorce our measurements of realistic fiction from our sense of the magnitude of this unconfessed and undischarged responsibility.

How should fiction order itself in this exigent and crucial situation? Its traditional and confident re.ort to all objectors would doubtless be: The Thing is true. Now truth is a great word and means a great thing, and the largeness of its service to mankind abundantly justifies its elevation into a law for conduct and a goal for science. But it is well to discriminate even in our worship of the worshipful. Truth avails only through its use or through its charm, and the idea that its usefulness is invariable is only a little less wild than the supposition that its charm is universal. Truth, in short, must be appraised by its consequences. There are facts which in moments of peril commanders withhold from their troops and governments from their peoples. No man would announce an only son's death to a mother at the turning point of typhoid fever. A man's faith in the primary and vital human values is part of his equipment for life; the same thing is equally true of a race: to rob man or race of that equipment is a wrong. It is a wrong particularly flagitious in a time of crisis when the remnant of hope and courage surviving in a racked world is its most valuable possession. "Respect the burden" is the law of generous spirits in every exigency. When the family is united and the wage is sure, a woman, in the frankness of conjugality, may call her husband a lazy and shiftless fellow, and remain, in her fashion, a good wife; she is not a good wife if she repeats the taunt on the morning when he goes to sea or into battle.

We talk of the morale of armies and of nations. The morale of the race is at stake, and if a large part of the most widely read literature is contributory to the disintegration of that morale, the literature in question must share the obloquy of the *défaitiste*. Obloquy only, not suppression; the bounds we set are destined for the critic, not the legislator. Let men see what they can, and say what they like, but let it be understood that the reception of their teaching must be gauged by its effect on the age-long undertakings of humanity. Many of these records are not facts, but if they are facts

THE IRRESPONSIBLE POWER OF REALISM

and are traitors to the ends for which we live, two courses are open to us; to give up those ends, a decision with which logic cannot quarrel, or to treat the facts summarily like other traitors. Half a man's manhood lies in the repudiation of certain valid grounds for fear and grief. Is the race's manhood gauged by other tests?

The above remarks may startle many readers; let us be quick to specify their limitations. The consideration of evil is a main part of the business known as life; its disclosure is inevitable and wise. What is wrong is the separation of the message from the hope, faith, and courage which impel us rationally to know the worse that we may seek the better. A brave man, in communicating disaster, communicates bravery, and the trembling balance is not wholly lost. Mrs. Wharton's *A Son at the Front* is a signal instance of sound equipoise; if the weight of the accumulated suffering is mountainous, the book is invincible in its hold on the faith that removes (or shoulders) mountains. M. Brieux is sunny even in his Tartarus. Mr. Galsworthy's objects are high; what is less helpful is the acrimony of his sorrow.

Again, the strongest distinction should be drawn between the facts that aid the will by the offer of new directions or new instigations to conduct and the facts—alleged or actual—that palsy or congeal the will. Everybody knows that evil abounds in the world, and the location and specification of that evil is a good. If an enemy exists, the man who tells you where the

enemy is, and how many guns he has, is a friend; but
he is not a friend who tells you that the enemy is invincible, unless he purposes by that assertion to prevent
the fight. Views which depreciate the worth of life and
man have no pertinence as guides to conduct; they
look to no remedial endeavor; they fail to voice even a
resolute and purposeful despair. Let art play its little
game with such pieces as its hand and eye approve —
let it play its game of bowls with death's-heads if it
please — but let it be told roundly that its game is a
game, and is no part of the tutelage or pilotage of a
straining race in its grapple with unparalleled adver-
sity.

V

Let us briefly summarize the argument. Realistic
fiction is art; as art, its place is high, valid, and secure.
It may employ truth as much as it will, provided that it
employs truth for art's sake. But the moment it employs truth for truth's sake it is on doubtful ground,
for truth, in the broad sense, cannot be effectually
served by any agency that looks to other ends than
truth. Truth is hard to reach when truth is the sole
object; what hope can there be in the results of a divided purpose? The combination of truth with untruth in a fabric whose end is unconcerned with truth
is perfectly legitimate; the combination of the purpose
of truth with any other purpose is unsound. The words
"beauty" and "goodness" have no place in the vocabulary of science. The attempt to be true and moral,

or to be true and immoral, warps the truth; the attempt to be true and artistic, to be true and beautiful, to be true and interesting, warps the truth. The things may coalesce, but the purposes cannot mingle. Realistic fiction, if we put aside its art, is pseudo-science, and its place in the twentieth century is a place cheek by jowl with alchemy and astrology. Nevertheless — so strange are the vagaries of a scientific age — it exercises as teacher a great and a totally irresponsible power, and it uses that power to a large extent for the emasculation of the race at an hour when the demands upon its manhood are superlative.

THE BONDAGE OF LIBERALITY

><<<<<<<<<<<<<<<<<<<<<<<<<<<<<

It is an odd thing that the liberal should have no more toleration for the conservative than the conservative for the liberal. The conservative has a right to his narrowness; an oak, which stands still, may logically as well as literally look down upon the moving sheep and bees and squirrels. But the liberal is by profession the man of differences, of the other idea, of two ideas, of ranging possibilities; neither the sheep nor the bee nor the squirrel scorns the oak. The liberal, whose door is open to ideas, should have a door that is open to conservative ideas. Criticism, which is liberality, should include criticism of one's self and of one's side. Yet this happens quite as rarely with the liberal as with the conservative. The Christian who bowing low before the statue of the discarded Jupiter asked the god to remember the courtesy if he should ever be restored to power is a man whom the liberal cordially despises. The man was doubtless calculating and two-faced; but, in that point at least, he was liberal. He was liberal enough to put a question to liberality.

I

Liberty is leave to do what we please. Liberalism is the state of mind which considers all ideas, which rejects only for reasons. Both these principles are of the highest value; yet, as is often the case with real superlatives, our estimates of both require correction. Let us turn first to liberty.

When liberty is absent and desired, when it is glorified by privation and longing, we come to speak of it almost as if it were an all-sufficing good. In a revolution or in a *risorgimento* men half believe that liberty is not merely liberty but is food and drink and house and goods and fellowship and art and science and diversion. It looks like a self-subsisting, independent good. Yet a moment's thought will show conclusively that liberty is only a conditional good, and that the condition which fixes its goodness is combined with a large number — with a formidably large number — of other things. A man may be an American and free, yet he will be full of trouble if the iceman does not visit him on the Fourth of July. What is liberty to a man when a coffin in the house incloses all that made it valuable? These are personal conditions, conditions which it might be hard or vain to universalize. But there are more general — more generally applicable — conditions which, lost in our contemplation of the supernal entity, we consider and analyze too little. In a world of grumbling freemen, subjects grumble because they are not free, and, possessed by one kindling thought, scarcely turn their thoughts to that combination of freedom with other requisites which is the true end of rational desire.

We are very ingenious in the fashion in which at

the same moment we set bounds to liberty and proclaim that the liberty which we have just pared and mulcted is unbounded. Liberty is leave to do what we please. But sometimes doing what we please is a bane to the community. The community withdraws this portion of our liberty from us, but, in withdrawing it, confers upon it a new name — license. The fiction that liberty is everywhere and always a benefit is maintained by the transparent verbal device of declaring that nothing which is not beneficial shall be called liberty. Last night we retrenched the royal prerogative; this morning we shout all the more lustily "God save the King."

Our inveterate habit of personification is responsible for a good deal of our confused idealism on this and kindred subjects. We never meet freedom as a person; her image, the Statue of Liberty, is more impotent than any serf. Freedom in practice is a state, a state which is never merely free but is many other things (rich, poor, young, old, wise, foolish) at the same time — a state in which, while present, its owner rarely sees anything particularly elevated or particularly satisfactory. He cannot worship freedom as she exists — as a state of mind or body in the concrete. But he must worship her, and to that end she must be made worshipful. What, then, shall he do? He abstracts and personifies. Abstraction, it is true, deadens; but personification enlivens; and since this person, of whom nothing but good is said by patriots and poets, is never subject to the disillusions of a personal encounter, he succeeds without much trouble in making it the object of a real, if somewhat misty, worship. Its distance and its cloudiness are its protection. The restrictions and disappointments he undergoes are all laid at the door of that earthly, plodding, homespun creature which is liberty as he knows it in daily life. He never dreams that the vision he danced with in a night of glamour at the ball is Cinderella.

There is good as well as evil in this doubleness. The positive fruits of liberty are probably worth all the sacrifices and exertions which the race pays for their acquirement, but it is also probable that the race could not have been impelled to those exertions and sacrifices without the spur of the illusion that those benefits were greater than they are. In this, as in other fields, man's unjustified expectations prompt him to justifiable endeavors. To a slothful man an adequate reward is often an inadequate incentive. But the entertainment of two conceptions of the same thing leads to confusion. We read Shelley's "Ode to Liberty" and Wordsworth's invocation of the "high-souled Maid" in whom the sea and the mountains found a listener, and we form a notion of liberty in its wholeness and its concentrated purity; whereas liberty as a fact, liberty as a help, exists only in parcels and in mixtures. Observation assures us of the comparative well-being of sundry nations in which liberty formed a wholesome partnership with knowledge, industry, and order; but poetry and sentiment, which are little affected by the plain merits of knowledge, industry, and order, persist in making over the whole profits of the undertaking to the most romantic and most prepossessing of the partners. It is hard to personify, and it is harder still to deify, a partnership (the Trinity, as everyone knows, has made unending trouble for its votaries).

Trouble, or at least confusion, arises when we seek to give to one ingredient of a combination the authority and significance which are really vested in the combination itself. We trust too much to mere liberty; we simplify the conditions of happiness; we take for granted the advent or the perpetuation of the associated factors. We handle truth as we have just now handled liberty. We abstract the quality and deify the abstraction. Even Thomas Henry Huxley, with his undeceivable practicality, writes of truth in the letter to Charles Kingsley as if truth had been not his utensil but his father or his God. The virtue of truth is not absolute and inherent but relative and conditional. In certain combinations which happen, for our benefit and for our deception, to be very frequent and usual combinations, truth is helpful to us; but its virtue lies in its consequences and its consequences are diverse. Knowledge mixes poisons and medicines almost in the same mortar; knowledge sharpens reaping-hooks and cutlasses on the same forge. The world has owed many of its hopes, its spurs, and its consolations to unproved and refutable illusions. Truth drives out the deities in order—finally—to accept the godhead; illusion in its breaking net enmeshes its destroyer.

In no place is this folly more manifest or more hurtful than in the romantic attitude toward love. Civilized man is a complex being; the grounds of his happiness must be complex. When he falls in love, he is prone to tell himself not that the ground of happiness has been complicated by the introduction of a new essential, but that it has been simplified by the substitution of a single new requirement for all the rest.

> Give me but what this ribband bound,
> Take all the rest the Sun goes round.

This is the phrase of courtly adulation, but it is also the cry of unreflecting passionate sincerity. The truth of course is that a man who has fallen in love today requires for happiness all that he required yesterday— and more. After the honeymoon he will resume his cigarette.

Between the dream of concentration and the rediscovery that diversity is inescapable, literature in its believing and its disbelieving moods moves like a pendulum. Lord Dunsany, curiously placed for once among the trusting idealists, sends his king at the close of *The Tents of the Arabs* to spend the throneless residue of his life in a little brown tent with the gipsy Eznarza. On the other hand, Mr. Maxwell Anderson in *Saturday's Children* re-enforces by a new instance the well-nigh proverbial wisdom of the doctrine that much besides love is essential to the happiness of marriage.

The mistake is a practical evil; couples marry, as in this play, in the faith that the largest factor in happiness is the whole. The slighted elements in the great complex that we call well-being revenge themselves. Mrs. Wharton, picturing a woman who had sacrificed reputation and society for love, puts the sad fact into unflinching and unerring words: "She had had what she wanted, but she had had to pay too much for it. She had had to pay the last bitterest price of learning that love has a price: that it is worth so much and no more."

The power of love to bestow happiness depends on its combination with other powers and assets which, in relation to the passion itself, are fortuities. It would have seemed that the study of this combination should have been among the foremost aims of knowledge. One face of the situation is visible to commercial wisdom; another to youthful passion. Both sides simplify too much; each evades the burden and the irritant of complexity. As with liberty, so with love; the worshiper of either can content himself with nothing less than the ascription of unlimited power over happiness to the object of his undivided homage. Once more worship, desirous of unity and perfection in its object, seeks to evade by a personification the grapple with an unesthetic and uninspiring aggregate of things. This simplified and glorified person supplies a mark toward which high feelings and fine phrases promptly gravitate. It is quite clear that all the glamour would vanish from a saying like

Men below and saints above
Say love is heaven and heaven is love,

if we felt ourselves bound to explain that the source of
superior happiness was not love in its quintessence but
Love and Company. The rhetoric as rhetoric is sound
enough; the only trouble is that it invades and infects
our thinking. Instead of studying the conditions which
enable Love to act as the almoner of Providence we
turn it into a quality and make that quality omnipotent.

In a well-known essay, "The Dissociation of Ideas,"
Remy de Gourmont points out the necessity of dis-
solving the imaginary cohesions of ideas, of severing
agglutinations which are not solidarities. This may be
wise counsel, but there is other work to be done in
the restoration of associations, of banded and united
qualities, for which our loosely personifying habits tend
to substitute the domination — almost the godship —
of a single trait. The unconjoined is the infertile;
bachelors and personifications should take notice.

II

I arrive now at the specific purpose of this essay,
which is the application of the above generality to the
liberal idea, the cult of liberalism and liberality. Es-
teeming liberty and love, I deprecate their worship as
abstractions; a like esteem and a like deprecation ac-
company me in my discussion of the liberal idea. That
idea arises in history, not as a self-sufficing, spheral unit,
but as a factor, a counterpoise, a qualification — almost
as a corrective or antidote. In that relation lies its virtue

and its health; insularity and simplification are its bane; as monolith it becomes cenotaph.

Liberalism is the trust in the other idea, the untried idea, the hope in difference, the reliance on tomorrow. Its vogue today is almost universal. Its strength as a party may seem to diminish, but that is the result of the appropriation of its principles by other parties who decline to wear its name. Radicalism is only liberalism at top speed, liberalism with the brakes off. The difference between conservatism and liberality is no longer the ancient logical difference between stability and motion; it is simply the difference between two rates of movement. They do much the same things, seek the same destination, but conservatism takes the later train. Conservatism in our time is procrastinating liberality. An avowed intention on the part of a government to confine itself to the original purposes of government, external security and internal order, would be held on all sides to be tantamount to abdication. Again, liberalism is perennially interesting, because motion attracts all eyes, and the permanent is almost another name for the invisible. Everybody's glance turns from the sentinel to the scout. For the establishment of democratic freedom, liberalism gets even more credit than the very large credit which it undoubtedly deserves, for the simple reason that its functions are self-advertising. Liberalism has bonds with science, and with a certain high type of religion. It saw in evolution a copy of itself in Nature, and no one could deny its kinship with the theism which saw in the progress of mankind successively clearer and higher manifestations of the divine principle.

Evolution is liberalism in the domain of nature, and there is an instructive analogy of an inexact but pointed kind between variation in a species and change or self-modification in a state or individual. A variation is an occurrence in a type; it is a deflection from the type, a deflection to which, in a few lucky cases, in the train of generations, the type itself capitulates and conforms. A variation is a heretic which finally converts the pope. Plainly the variation (or heretic) cannot do its work without a type (or pope) to work upon. Modification can act only upon the modifiable, and the modifiable includes — in certain of its sides and aspects — the permanent. "Brooke is very pulpy," says the sagacious Humphrey Cadwallader in *Middlemarch*. "You can run him into any mold, but you cannot keep him in any mold." It is impossible to modify the shape of a smoke-wreath or of a foam-wreath, though both the smoke-wreath and the foam-wreath are subject to facile and unbounded variation. They offer to no variation a chance to infix and standardize itself.

Darwin held that the useful variations were commonly slight; differences became considerable — i.e., types were modified — only by accumulation. A rodent is born with a new slant to its ear, a new curve to its jaw. Evolution grasps at the difference. But in nineteen points out of twenty, perhaps in ninety-nine of a hundred, this rodent is a copy of its parents and its ancestors. These nineteen or ninety-nine points are adjustments, commodities, securities, quite as much as the adventurous variation. Even in this exceptional creature, who is evolution's lucky throw and priceless opportunity, the type, or sum of the conformities, is far more powerful and — to the creature itself — far more useful than the variation. The type, faithful, stereotyped, unassuming steward and protector, keeps the animal alive, while evolution in its part of specialist refracts its ear or realigns its jaw. The type is dominant in still another way. The useful difference has not succeeded, evolution has not scored — until the variation has inscribed itself in the norm. The norm or type is the album, the compilation, in which Nature has assembled her variations for safe-keeping. That which resists is as indispensable as that which assaults, because, when the day is won, that which resists is that which consummates and fixes.

Even in evolution itself, therefore, variation can do nothing until it has converted its opponent into its ally. The effectual thing is not variation, but a combination in which variation is important. The radical leans on the forces which he berates; he spends his days in abusing the state and his nights in dreaming of the premiership.

III

Liberalism is open-mindedness, the faith in the alternative, in the *other* way of doing or thinking.

Obviously, if there are two ways of living, it is well for all of us to know that there are two ways, and to choose the better. But it is equally obvious that, in a world in which mere existence is a triumph, the *first* business of life is to discover a single way — any way — in which it can outwit its vigilant and diverse enemies. Man is born into a world of habits and customs which, to the eyes of the latter-day liberal, take on the semi-comic guise of fetishes, conventions, mummeries, but which earlier times viewed, and often justly viewed, as fences, guarantees, provisions. The personal routine, the social order, into which a man is born is the rope thrown from the deck to the sailor struggling in the waves; he has no mind to finger rescue critically, to be captious in his scrutiny of ropes; safe on the deck, two days or two hours later, he may exercise the niceties of choice. Life to early peoples is a continuous emergency, and emergencies are uncritical of means. A primitive tribe feels that its life depends on its adhesion to the one system of habits which experience — recorded in tradition — has indorsed; it depends also on the force with which it can impress upon the minds of youth the necessity of perpetuating that tradition. At first this force is one of habit or custom; later on, as the mind emerges, its energy is re-embodied in beliefs.

To that belief as to the system it reflects and re-enforces the race clings like the imperiled sailor to his rope; the energy of the clutch is all-important. But time passes; the race matures; its resources and its securities augment. It learns finally that two courses may be possible; it learns also that the untried course may be the wiser of the two. It discards one belief and adopts another. The admission that one belief is wrong involves the admission that belief as such is fallible. Logically, it should diminish the certainty of all convictions. Liberalism and skepticism should have slept — or waked — in the same cradle. There should have been two great coinciding moments in the history of the origin of both: the discovery that a man could differ from his neighbor, and the discovery that he could change, i. e., that he could differ from himself. The fallibility of the species was implicit in the first of these discoveries; his own was implicit in the second.

The subsidence of conviction should have been the logical result, but logic, the hare, has a celerity with which psychology, the cripple, finds it hard to keep pace. The discovery that belief might be misleading did not, I think, in the first instance have much effect upon the vigor of belief. The certainty of a man's belief, even in our own day, depends much more upon his appetite for certainty than upon the sufficiency or insufficiency of its grounds. Convictions are rather visceral than cerebral, and the deep bass of the constitution with its masterful "So be it" drowns out the brain's slighter tenor with its piercingly reiterant *Que sçais-je?* A man in an incorrupt era grasps an idea almost as he grasps a mallet or a rudder or a scythe. The advent of liberalism, the perception of a second possibility, alters opinion here and there without modifying the habit, the tenacity, of conviction. The new idea is identified with the old group, the sacred band of prehistoric and unbending certainties.

What saves a man is the strength of his belief in relevant and valid objects. The extension of that strength to the largest number of relevant and valid objects is an obvious desideratum. Any bar to that extension is an evil. The removal of any such bar is gain. Liberalism removes the bar of prejudice and superstition; it permits the extension of the primary force of belief to new and valid objects. These objects, being new, are interesting; they arouse the prick of curiosity and the spur of acquisition; we are grateful to the force that renders them accessible. But liberalism is a derivative and conditional, not a primary and absolute, good; like liberty, like love, like other traits, it is a partner in a serviceable combination.

As with love and liberty, however, we tend, by a sleight of hand called personification, to take liberalism out of this combination, to treat it like an insulated self-sufficient force, and to transfer the homage from the federation to the individual. We begin to worship, not the right to change, but change itself. First of all, we are more interested in the novelty of the objects to which the primary vigor of belief is to be applied than in their validity or relevance. Next, we apply that vigor to new objects without asking if they be valid or relevant or not. Lastly, we apply our minds to the new objects without minding whether vigor of belief or even reality of belief sustains the application. The means, the symbol, the condition, has supplanted the reality or end; the wafer has become the sacred body.

IV

We have seen that skepticism reaches back to the very origins of progress. The whole edifice metaphorically trembles when the first decayed block in its foundation or its roof has been extracted and replaced. Not only is the precedent subversive, but the aperture itself is a convenience and an incitement toward removal. The surface of life is full of promptings to reflection. Two parties, turn by turn, govern England for a century; under both England suffers, flourishes, and lasts. A simple fact like this is a blow to partisanship. Macaulay, a convinced party man, but also a historian, said that probably the best men in the two parties that had so long divided England were the men who were closest to the common frontier. A Chinese traveler, visiting America, observes the pointless diversities of Christianity. Would not a thoughtful Baptist or Episcopalian whom chance threw into his way admit that the smile with which the traveler viewed our discords was still more philosophical than Asiatic? Convictions as mere beliefs tend to be impaired with each new discovery of the extent to which diversities of belief are compatible with intellect and gravity. If men had been pure intelligences, they would have become pure skeptics at a comparatively early stage of civilization. Fortunately conviction is sustained by stronger forces than intelligence.

The vigor of an unspoiled race finds many ways of circumventing the impulsions toward uncertainty. The variety of philosophies leads to doubt; but if comparison brings doubt, combination may restore to certainty; conviction, losing its hold on particulars, retrieves its vigor by a newborn faith in synthesis. Extremity in opposed beliefs may sap our faith in all beliefs, or it may simply sap our faith in all extremes, actually reenforcing for the time being our faith in middle terms or arbitrations. When a powerful and long-dominating creed is attacked, the first attacks are made on its circumference. Conviction may actually profit for a time by the withdrawal of the scattered energy of belief from a hundred indefensible and relatively unimportant outposts, and its concentration on a few nearer, worthier, and more inspiring objects. The reverence which a whole pantheon could not command is directed toward the single deity who supplants it.

The will to believe, if strong enough, will find new objects, will even for a space extract vigor from its perils and discouragements. But in the sequel the new defenses turn out to be as penetrable as the old. A synthesis, as Emerson has convincingly shown in "The Method of Nature," may share the partiality of its own constituents. The theory that truth is always in the mean may turn out finally to be itself extreme. The concentration of love and reverence on fewer and larger objects may draw after it a concentration of scrutiny, of critical attention, which detects breaches in the inner wall. The Turk, satisfied for a time with Asia Minor, will creep on toward Constantinople. We come to hold all things with a proviso. We become capable of temporary, tentative adhesion to almost any belief which shall present us with the *visée* of novelty; we become incapable of security, of constancy, in any belief.

Liberalism stands for freedom; it comes from the same stem as liberty. But freedom, for an active thing, means freedom to act. To act usefully is to act with vigor and decision. Now, if you free the mind at the cost of its power to act with vigor and decision, you have, as it were, freed your captive bird by pulling its compressed body through the wires of its cage with a violence that has shattered both its wings. Two things—two of those half reconcilable, half irreconcilable contradictories in which reality abounds—are necessary to the effectiveness of mind. These things are firmness and plasticity. In the long early centuries when firmness overbalances plasticity, liberalism is the savior and the guide. When plasticity increases, when it equals, when it finally surpasses firmness, its value, though receding, continues to be great. But there comes a time when the excess of plasticity over firmness reaches a point which is destructive of the virtues of both qualities.

That point has been reached in many minds in our

own era; it has been reached on several momentous topics. Not in the majority of minds, as majorities are reckoned by the census-taker; not on the majority of topics, as topics are viewed by the compilers of encyclopedias. But the topics affected are precisely those on which guidance, instruction, confidence are indispensable; and the minds affected are that small but powerful group to which the perplexed world turns for precept and example. I do not mean to affirm that leaders invariably lack convictions: George Santyana is convinced; Benedetto Croce is convinced. Men of this kind readily put faith in the ideas which they originate; there is no argument for truth or untruth so powerful as discovery. What is needed is the power to impart or infix these convictions, or — shifting the responsibility — the capacity in others to receive them. William James had the sound type of mind, the type that can originate in case of need, and that can *appropriate* with energy. The power to retain convictions for a lifetime in a swaying world and to impress those convictions upon others has given to the Humanism of Paul Elmer More and Dr. Babbitt an importance that is quite real and another importance that is factitious. Instability felt and resented the tacit stricture in this constancy; the vane on the turret naturally feels that the turret is brutally insensible to the fluctuations of the weather.

Liberalism has been a great good; it is still a good for many races; it is still a good for many persons and some classes in peoples for whom as a whole it has ceased to be a good; it may become a great good, perhaps the supreme means to good, in the uncertain future. For the time being, however, in the field of the individual mind (for I do not here take up the tangled question of liberalism in the state), it has overdone its own work; it has swept aside its own dams like a stream, and, in so doing, has swept aside the securities for its own good behavior. The world is saved by the largest possible choice among alternatives to one of which, after inspection and decision, it is prepared unflinchingly and stoutly to adhere. It is lost if the extension of the range of choice unsettles the capacity to decide and to fulfill.

THE SERMON ON THE MOUNT
ITS RATIONAL BASIS

THE Sermon on the Mount has had some very strong extra-rational supports. It has had on its side the will of God, the word of Christ, the bidding of the Church. Even with these powerful sanctions, its boldest doctrines have often seemed extravagant, have commonly been ignored in practice, by the very persons who most reverenced its guarantors. How, then, must those doctrines appear in an age which permits itself to doubt, and even to deny, the soundness of its guarantees? It is assumed, almost without investigation, that any other sanctions are impossible, that a basis in reason for non-worshipers is out of the question for doctrines which worshipers have practically held to be unreasonable. To seek to prove that reason, quite apart from God or Christ, might arrive at the same conclusions as the texts enjoining unselfishness in the Sermon on the Mount will seem to most rationalists a bold, even a foolhardy, undertaking. Yet that is exactly what I am trying to prove in the present essay. I reach much the same conclusions, but I pause there; as will be seen in the sequel, I do not turn these conclusions into precepts, into injunctions, with the same readiness and fearlessness as the author of the Sermon on the Mount.

The self-regarding instincts in human nature are very general — not to say universal — and very strong; that is a fact, and, like every momentous fact, it will occupy a large place in the mind of every rational observer and assessor of human nature. It is easy to pass from doubts of the wisdom of the believers in general disinterestedness to doubts of the wisdom of disinterestedness. It is not hard to imagine that selfishness is rational because the acknowledgment of its presence is so. But it is clear that the same type of analogy would make folly rational, for it is hard to dispute the assertion of Dr. Stockmann that most people are foolish. It may be highly rational for Peter to expect Paul to do things which it is highly irrational for Paul to do. To tell the idealist who offers himself as a physician for the commonwealth that he will get no patients is one thing; it is quite another to tell him that his remedies are frauds.

The passages in the Sermon on the Mount at which it is conceivable that reason might arrive without subsidy from deity or Christ may be exemplified in two outstanding dicta:

Therefore all things whatsoever ye would that men should do to you, do ye even so to them: for this is the law and the prophets. (Matthew 7:12.)

Ye have heard that it hath been said, Thou shalt love thy neighbour, and hate thine enemy.

But I say unto you, Love your enemies, bless them that curse you, do good to them that hate you, and pray for them which despitefully use you and persecute you. (Matthew 5:43-44.)

The first of these two verses, with its "Do ye even so to them," practically abolishes the difference (so immeasurable to our mere instincts) between Self and other people. It practically sets up a Self, one's own Self, another Me, in every other person, and it boldly insists that the Self or Me in every other person shall be treated with exactly the same respect and affection as the Self that is housed in one's own person. This principle is called unselfishness. It might equally well be called *all-Self-hood*. In effect, it locates the Self at every conscious point in the universe.

The two other verses are simply an extension and consequence of this principle. Since the Self, our Self, is everywhere, it follows that it is in our enemies, in those who curse us, hate us, use us despitefully, and persecute us. In them it is as powerful and sacred as in every other quarter.

Now putting aside all notions of infallibility, of authority, of Christhood and godship, let us ask ourselves what would be the attitude of an unlimited, pure intelligence toward these propositions in the Sermon on the Mount. I have elsewhere defined morality as simply the conduct which a realization of all the facts would produce in an unprejudiced being. Let us, accordingly, ask ourselves what would be the attitude of an unprejudiced, perfectly informed intelligence toward the propositions we have quoted.

It seems clear that for an unprejudiced mind all Selves as Selves would be equally significant. As units of consciousness, they might differ in value as they differed in intensity or elevation; but these variations would be altogether unrelated to their attachment to this or that specific center. One pocket may contain ten dollars, another ten cents, but their usefulness as pockets might be equal. "All men are equal before the law"; because the law, in this instance, attempts to identify itself with absolute and unconfined intelligence. The Sermon on the Mount equalizes men; it recognizes that Self is a prejudice. Absolute reason does exactly the same thing; only, having no Self, it has no prejudice to overcome and acts from the start on the premise of equality.

I have said that absolute reason can do this. But something far, far inferior to absolute reason, something no better and no other than ordinary human nature, can do precisely the same thing whenever it is in a situation that inhibits bias. A judges between B and C. He assumes in this judgment that the abstract claims of B and C are equal. B, judging between A and C, would assign the same equality to A and C. C would make precisely the same assumption the basis of his arbitration between A and B. Now put these three points together, and is it not plain that, assuming their correctness, we arrive at the conclusion that A, B, and C are equal, and that if A, judging between himself and B, cannot perceive the equality, his failure is simple deficiency of understanding? The Sermon on the Mount puts all men on an equal basis; absolute reason does precisely the same thing; even ordinary human nature, when it acts without bias, ranges itself unhesitatingly on the side of absolute reason and the Sermon on the Mount.

In a democratic age most organizations are conducted on the supposition that the welfare of one man is just as important as the welfare of every other. A man's comfort may be worth fifty times as much to him as the comfort of anybody else, yet he cheerfully, and often eagerly, allies himself with associations on the understanding that his importance and that of his neighbor shall be adjusted in the pacific ratio of one to one. Momentous as our own dinner is, we content ourselves with the same helping as our neighbor. In government we give or affect to give the same rights to everybody. Everybody is supposed to obtain the same goods for the same price from the same merchant. Even in literary and athletic competitions, where the desire is to elicit and to emphasize inequalities, we insist on equal chances for unequal powers. In social intercourse it is agreed that self-assertion is impossible; and the comedy of self-subordination is practiced with gusto in the politest circles.

The above illustrations are so obvious that I risk the charge of falling into the commonplace. The enforcement of such points would be ridiculous; there is ground for fear that even the enumeration may be tiresome. Yet the Sermon on the Mount is accused of paradox for nothing more or less than pushing these commonplaces to their rational completion—for acting thoroughly and consistently on the principle that one's Self and everybody else are entitled to exactly the same measure of consideration. It is true that we are very timid and lazy in extending our applications of the idea, and that novelty or boldness in the extension of a favorite and familiar principle frightens us almost as much as if our entire conduct were governed by an antithetic theory and practice. When Peer Gynt and the ship's cook, struggling in the water, both lay their hands upon a floating object which is capable of supporting only one, Peer Gynt thrusts the cook by force into the water. That is another principle, a very popular principle, a principle to which most of us, in the fields of business, politics, and international relations, are decisively, if not very eagerly or heartily, committed. I suppose most people would say that the fundamental relation between man and man was that between the ship's cook and Peer Gynt; the rest is truce or play or affectation. Nevertheless, if Peer Gynt and the cook, on shore, as informed and impartial spectators, had seen two other persons in the aforesaid situation, they would have felt that the claims of both to help, to life, to pity, and to regret were equal. Would this attitude be rational? We have virtually answered that question in calling it impartial. All that the Sermon on the Mount does is to suggest that they take this rationality with them into the water.

The difficulty of sacrificing life to an abstraction is obvious, and, even where rationality asks less, special difficulties confront us in any attempt at private obedience to its less usual precepts. Equality at a dinner, equality in a polling-place, is made easy for us by a preconcerted understanding that in those surroundings the distribution of advantages is to be made on the supposition that everybody else is worth as much and worthy of as much as we are. Since this is the accepted and prevalent view, participation on our part calls for nothing more virile than assent; the real hardship would consist in refusal. The Self, the greedy, exorbitant Self, is controlled by a pre-existent force — the social pact — outside the Self. All that is relatively easy. But the Sermon on the Mount refuses to content itself with this restriction of the scope of reason to areas where reason has convention at its back. It goes much further. It says that even where, as in business and the mutualities of states, society unleashes the Self, cries "Havoc," and lets loose the dogs of war, the Self must be its own leash, must itself assume the responsibility for the maintenance of that rational, impartial point of view, which society in this instance declines to guarantee.

Let us now turn to the other famous and arduous injunction: "But I say unto you, Love your enemies, bless them that curse you, do good to them that hate you, and pray for them which despitefully use you and persecute you." This appears to many thoughtful and well-meaning people to be an infraction, almost a defiance, of common sense. Is it possible to put such a doctrine on a non-Christian, non-theistic, purely intellectual basis?

Ignorance when it suffers is angry; anger is medicinal. Since it cannot decently be angry without a pretext, it presumes guilt and imagines evil in the source, human or nonhuman, of its suffering. These assumptions justify in its eyes the hatred, curses, and injuries to which it is impelled by dominating instincts. But the instant knowledge and intelligence supervene, they begin to restrict the permissible area of hatred, injury, and malediction, and the conclusion and consummation of their work would lead them to the state of mind so tersely and trenchantly indicated by the Sermon on the Mount.

A child is angry with the pin that accidentally pricks it, with the scalding drop of water that falls by inadvertence on its flesh. Knowledge comes with time, and resentment is diminished or dispelled. A tramp curses a mosquito; a man of sense, even in destroying the mosquito, knows that the insect is as guiltless as the drop of water or the pin. A thoughtless man hates the carnivorous animal which satisfies its hunger with his flesh; a philosopher in the jaws of a crocodile or the coils of a boa constrictor would not hate the animal who simply imitates his own unresentful conduct toward unoffending oxen, sheep, and chickens. Put savage man in place of savage beast; for crocodile or boa constrictor, write Dyak or Comanche. Will not the wise man see at once that, just as he was half beast in his hatred of the beast, so he is half savage in his rancor toward the savage? He *should* resist; he *may* destroy: but in neither case would a perfectly sane man allow his acts to color his emotions.

Let us pass from savagery to civilization. The crimes in civilized societies are largely perpetrated, as the cant names Mohawks and Apaches show, by an unassimilated savage remnant lingering in the bypaths of enlightened states. Like the cruder savage, they must be restrained; like the cruder savage, are they not entitled to exemption from vindictiveness and rancor? A man strikes us on the face; we retort with furious hand or tongue. But knowledge intervenes. The man is crazed. Resentment ceases. The man is drunk. Resentment hesitates. The man, by place and race, by birth and wont, is criminal. But crime is often either madness or disease. Is either madness or disease the object of a wise man's ire or truculence?

Every act that has a source or an echo or even a double in consciousness must be a link in a causal series; if so, it must be inevitable. What is the attitude of intelligence toward the inevitable in mind or matter? A wise man will put the destructiveness of a human criminal, the destructiveness of a Bengal tiger, and the destructiveness of Vesuvius on exactly the same footing. When an injury is done me, my first impulse is to rage; my second to inquire if I have the right to be angry, or, in other words, if I could expect to be upheld and encouraged in my anger by nineteen-twentieths of my acquaintance. At this point investigation tends to halt; but if I go a step further, if I ask myself, putting my claims altogether on one side, what actually took place in the mind of the assailant, the result is invariably the same — a marked diminution in the liveliness of my hostility. I have no doubt that, if I knew all, and were completely subject to reason, not a trace of hostile feeling would remain. Let us even suppose that the adversary is malicious. (Malice is a fact in human nature, and therefore a possibility in the given instance.) Even so, if for his malice as I imagined it in the first fervors of retaliation, I substitute malice as I myself have felt it in earlier and different relations, appeasement is the instantaneous result. When I am angry with people, I am not superlatively cruel; when I wish evil to people, the evil that I wish is not so very great. If he wronged my neighbor, I should govern and retrench my wrath, and the duty of wisdom is to grasp the fact that I am to my aggressor no better and no larger than my neighbor is to me.

Knowledge is the best of specifics. The question of Lamb, " How could I hate him if I did know him?" — almost too hackneyed for citation — is big with the consoling implication that ignorance is the parent of ill will. It is likewise parent of heartlessness. Nora Helmer, begging Torvald to find a place in the bank for Mrs. Linden, and yet not to dismiss the troublesome

Krogstad, says ingenuously, "But instead of Krogstad, you could dismiss some other clerk." So enormous a heartlessness almost implies an equally enormous innocence, or rather both innocence and heartlessness are grounded on simple ignorance, ignorance of the primary and axiomatic fact that an unknown person is a human being. "I *cannot* do harm to one whom I *know!*" cries the upholder of the Vikings, Hilda Wangel. Ten minutes of intimate conversation with a broken and tottering woman have robbed her of the impulse and the power to appropriate that woman's husband. In war we tell lies about the enemy — admitting by that practice that the truth would reconcile or soften us. It is well known that the slightest personal contact of a nonmilitary kind between soldiers of hostile camps leads to the sudden surprised, half-joyous, half-ashamed discovery that the adversary we have hated is a fable. Hostile clans, through the very identity of their habits, their psychology, and their standards, are often closer to each other than to any foreigner or neutral, and this likeness, which division and contention have increased, is a preparation for understanding and even for friendliness, if the slightest chance for mutual acquaintance is afforded. Romance, which in this case seems to prop itself on reason, would almost have us think that two chiefs of warring clans are in a position closely resembling that of two actors, good friends offstage and on the stage, but cast by accident for the parts of Hotspur and Prince Henry, of Carlos and Hernani. When they meet by peaceful accident or truce in combat, each recognizes his Self in the other, and in that recognition hatred vanishes.

When every man sees in his fellow his *possible* Self or much more than his *necessary* Self in a given situation, when, in short, a man has the *facts* in his grasp, he moves in the path ordained and prefigured in the Sermon on the Mount. When Cleopatra strikes in the face the messenger whose only offense is the announcement of the simple fact that Antony is married to Octavia, and declares

> Thou shalt be whipp'd with wire, and stew'd in brine,
> Smarting in lingering pickle.

we perceive that the sovereign of Egypt is not only a termagant but a fool. When Fantine in *Les Misérables* spits in the mayor's face, and we are told in the fewest and quietest words possible that "M. Madeleine wiped his face," we realize that this is more than sainthood — it is wisdom. Let sheer intelligence reach a certain point, and this is the inevitable outcome. "Forgive them, for they know not what they do." The logic of that is as unsurpassable as its magnanimity.

To sum up the two lines of argument. Every man is one, counts as one. In democracies that is the recognized basis of civic life. The Sermon on the Mount merely says that it should likewise be the basis of the personal life, and the mild axiom suddenly puts on the grisly aspect of a paradox. Again, every man, in all he does, does what he must, and no man is to be abused, hated, or disliked for anything he does, though, if the thing be bad, he may and must be cut off from the possibility of repeating it. I have not taken up in this essay the discussion of the injunctions to offer the other cheek, to give the cloak to the taker of the coat, to walk two miles with the man who has compelled us to walk one. I think that conduct in these cases should be governed by the principles that rule the former cases, but I think the application in these later instances calls for fuller treatment than is possible within my present limits. A man may serve the commonwealth; a man may be disabled by two blows on the cheek. It is not clear that a man who would and should protect the commonwealth from the loss of any other useful servant should disown the obligation merely because that servant is himself. Is the world better served by his retention, or his abandonment of the coat or cloak? What else would he be doing in the half hour or hour that he declines to spend in accompanying the pedestrian who makes booty of his time? Either answer, yes or no, to these entangled questions leaves the principle intact; indeed the principle itself is the referee to furnish the decision.

There is another aspect of the problem which calls for fuller and more careful scrutiny. Let us assume that we know the course which entire knowledge and supreme intelligence would counsel in a given situation. Does anything remain but to follow that course to the height of our capacity and in contempt of every fear and prejudice? Ordinarily there could be but a single answer to this question; but if the prejudice were basic, if it were not only mental but organic, if it were bedded in the tissues, if it had been part of every instinct and every motive that had prompted action since our birth, if our whole efficiency, almost our whole being, were ribbed and fenced and bastioned with this prejudice, we should have to think twice before we treated it as nonexistent. That is precisely what has happened in the case of the Self. Every man is appointed and committed by the constitution of his physical and moral being to the guarding and cherishing of a particular item of consciousness which he describes by the intimate, but evasive, name of Self. Self is a searchlight throwing into intense distinctness for one person a minute tract of conscious life which is generally no larger, no better, no more significant to the universe, or worthier of exceptional illumination than any other tract. "A hand's breadth of it stands alone in the bare miles round about." Here is the great anomaly. The organism — the tiny, gasping, fleeting, powerless organism — flings down its gauntlet to the irresistible planet, and declares, "I am the world."

The Self is a prejudice. Self-love is an error. A preference which nobody else shares must obviously be a delusion. Yet, plainly, we here confront a prejudice that differs *toto caelo* from — we will say — a prejudice against olives or a prejudice against bobbed hair. Nature, by a fiat which we cannot revoke or resist, has chosen to put into the hands of this indefensible, but ineradicable, prejudice the motive force of individual and social life. Unselfishness even before it can lift a finger must get a Self to preach it. Strike out the love of Self, put in its place a theory or a standard that affirms that the affections of every man shall be parceled out in equal lots between himself and his equally significant fellows, and the urgency behind the cosmos that we know is gone. Look at the thing from the point of view of physiology. Consciousness is the efflux of a brain; its every act is the consequence of an act of that brain. This brain is the exclusive possession and agent of a particular body, a body by which it is inclosed, generated, guarded, and fed. Imagine this brain, and the consciousness which is its outflow, converted into the impartial agent and undistinguishing servitor of the billion or more of minds and bodies that are classified as human. This is exactly what a minute ago we discovered to be reasonable, the attitude which would be approved and shared by an all-wise, impartial being surveying the universe from a segregated pinnacle. Yet now, looked at from the organic point of view, this high sanity takes on an aspect of absurdity. "Thou hast bidden me to destroy my master," said the obedient but finally rebellious genie to the too grasping Aladdin. Consciousness, whose master is the brain, which is itself the servant of the body, might make a like reply to the undaunted Sermon on the Mount.

Wisdom must reckon with all the facts. The equal value of all men (more precisely of all equal quantums or amounts of sensibility) is one fact. The illusion of each one of a billion and a half of human units that his own being is the capital and supreme fact in the organic universe is another. We cannot impose obligations of unselfishness upon men without reference to the fact that all their primary instincts and many of their acquired habits point in the exactly opposite direction. Laws must be controlled in part by the capacity for obedience, and the capacity for obedience, in its turn, by the correspondence of those laws to the nature and predispositions of the subject. This is the occasion for the remark in the first paragraph of this essay to the effect that in our day it was impossible to turn conclusions into precepts with the fearless readiness of the unshrinking Sermon on the Mount.

The difficulty is great, but the opposition between the facts, though considerable, is by no means so extensive or uncompromising as the opposition between the principles. Selfishness and unselfishness are polar opposites, but Self and Non-Self are only intermittently and incidentally hostile. The willingness to sacrifice the other man's life to my own appetite for dinner may be abominable, but it will become operative only in the comparatively exceptional case when dinner by any other means is unattainable. Quite as often — indeed, in time of peace much more often — the other man, the Non-Self, is a convenience, a source, a comfort, a diversion, and I have exactly the same motives for cherishing him that I have for preserving any other diversion, comfort, convenience, or resource. Under favorable conditions self-interest and disinterestedness often prescribe exactly the same thing. A carpenter builds a house. He wills to build the house; it is his shortest path to bread and clothing. But the building of the house is precisely what the world would have him do if the world were infinitely selfish and he were its slave. As long as this agreement lasts, the verbally startling fact that every man is a mote in every other man's consciousness and a universe in his own does not bring about the smallest strife or trouble. The two paradoxes — each a paradox from the other's point of view — lie down as amicably together as the lion and the lamb under the soothing lullabies of Jewish prophecy. No combination could be happier; none shows the world in a more encouraging or friendly light. Behind the disinterested act lie all the momentum of self-interest; behind, or rather in front of, the self-seeking impulse lies all the beneficence of self-forgetfulness.

The ideal would plainly consist in the universality of this combination, and in this universality morality, so far as the Self and the Non-Self are involved, would disappear. But there are large and significant fields of life in which the interest of Self and neighbor are opposed, in which a man gains by his brother's loss. This is the point where the two principles join battle. Shall a boy take the apple which he and the other boy want? Shall a man take the job which he and the other man want? Shall he take the trade which he and the other man want? Shall he take the prize which he and his competitor desire? Dare we say, not merely to Plato and Emerson, but to Quivis or Aliquis and What's-his-name, that the boundary line between Self and Non-Self is to be obliterated? Dare we follow the common voice of the Sermon on the Mount and of enlightened and impartial reason, and say to the man in the street that harm is harm, whether it falls to me or you, that weal is weal, whether it be yours or mine, that the object of both our lives is to increase the good *anywhere,* to lessen the evil *anywhere,* without reference to the location of that evil or that good on this or that side of the abandoned and abolished frontier of the Self? "Thy necessity is greater than mine," said fallen Sidney, passing the water flask to the fallen private soldier on the field of Zütphen — simply putting, with an incredible simplicity, the two necessities side by side, and noting the preponderance. We cherish that incident not unjustly as an honor to human nature, but it is no less certainly a disgrace to human nature that its rarity should have made it memorable. The world applauds, disclaiming or renouncing imitation.

It will doubtless be said that evolution, to which we owe most of our progress, is the consequence of every creature's overwhelming and absorbing desire to sustain its life and to reproduce its kind, and that if every diatom and protozoan had loved its neighbor as itself, we should probably in 1930 have nothing but diatoms and protozoa, if indeed these exalted species had not been extinguished by their magnanimity. It may be said with some truth that it is the barbarous struggle for existence which has enabled certain races or classes to survive, to gain power, to gain leisure, to poeticize, to philosophize, and so, finally, to attain a point of vantage which disdains and reprehends the struggle for existence. All this is true, and its claim to emphasis should not be disregarded. But it must not be forgotten that evolution in this matter is two-faced. Evolution teaches the cell self-sacrifice, or, at least, self-subordination, that it may teach the organism self-defense and self-assertion. Evolution teaches the citizen self-conquest and self-surrender that it may fortify a solidified and compact state for conflict with its rivals. Every man who finds in his own soul nothing but the self-subserving instinct should learn from the structure of his own body by how many mutualities and reciprocities that towering and avid Ego is sustained. Evolution is a sort of Bonaparte, patronizing both Christianity and massacre. Its methods improve with its products; for aught we know, evolution itself may evolve. The ethics of the Sermon on the Mount, therefore, do not necessarily find any insuperable obstacle in the theory of evolution.

It may be said that the doctrine, whether opposed to evolution or not, is opposed to the type of human nature for which evolution is responsible. Sacrifice implies the conquest of nature, and the loss of whatever power lay in the volition of the conquered. There is force in this view, but for the instant let us limit discussion to the remark that, if sacrifice is exacted of me, it is likewise exacted of all others for my sake, and that dividends are as inseparable from the regimen as assessments. Moreover, it is difficult to do justice to the waste of energy involved in competition and in conflict. View human energy as a single instrument; view human welfare as a single end; adopt as the ideal the utilization of every particle of that energy for that end — surely no utopian or fantastic ideal, since it is realized, in a fashion, in every deer and every falcon. (The only difference is that we are viewing the human beings as a species.) Why not let exactly the same thing happen that would happen if the species were an individual? As things now stand, the division of mankind into persons results in the simple throwing away of immeasurable quantities of this power through its use in the contentions of these individuals with each other.

Two seafaring nations face each other without a pound of naval armament on either side. Zero equals zero, and zero cannot frighten zero. They are equal, and are, in a sort, secure. Each builds a million tons of hostile shipping. The cost is enormous, and the equality and security remain exactly what they were before. When war, on earth and sea, takes place, all the energy put forth by the defeated party is lost to the welfare of the species. But that is not all. All the energy put forth by the victor in overcoming the exertions of the vanquished is likewise lost to the welfare of the species. The victor has paid this huge price for the mere chance to set about doing something really useful even to itself. Perhaps it can now feed its subjects on the wheat grown in the lands of the conquered enemy. The great fortunes, the supreme offices, are achieved by few, but they are sought by many, and, speaking generally, the energy expended on the contest by the unsuccessful many is wasted. The sum of human capacity, at best, seems to fall painfully short of the aggregate of human needs. *Waste in shortage* is the most insane and unforgivable of errors. We are sailors on half rations in a boat in mid-ocean, and half the biscuit at which we recklessly and angrily snatch falls overboard into the sea.

These are arguments of real weight, yet it is possibly in this very point of the economy of power that the thesis of the Sermon on the Mount and of absolute reason is most vulnerable to attack. The Self is not an accident, nor a mistake. It is a product of evolution — evolution whose frugality can waste nothing. It exists, if we dare not now say to a purpose, at least to an end. The Self is on exactly the same footing as an arm, a tusk, a fin, a horn, a gland, or a knee joint. It would be vain to contend that any one of these acquirements is useless. The least unreasonable affirmation conceivable would be that the Self, like certain organs in the body, has outlived its usefulness, and that its inflammation, like that of an appendix, is becoming a menace to the life and comfort of the organism. Nobody in our time, however, will be likely to take even this carefully guarded proposition. The Self is a battery, a battery of quite unequaled force, and it is far better to enlist its energy on the side of beneficence than to trust to any other battery which disinterestedness may be able to contrive for its own purposes. Great as the waste of power now is, the waste of power under a system which attempted to substitute an equal interest in everybody for a predominant interest in Self might be much greater; the economy might be of the sort which saves at the spigot and wastes at the bunghole. The whole trick of the cunning workman evolution has been to get the cell or the Self to find its own good in the good of the organism or the body politic or economic of which it constitutes a minor part.

The injunction "Love your neighbor as yourself" is perfectly sound as an indirect or symbolic expression of the equal significance of all men before the eyes of an all-seeing and unbiased intelligence. But its value as a precept is more questionable. Assuming the amount of psychic force at man's command to remain unaltered, how could he love his neighbor as himself without loving himself a good deal less than he now does? Benevolence, like self-love, has only twenty-four hours in its day, and the division of its kind acts or kind thoughts among a billion and a half of souls would result in fractions of unrealizable and unmanageable smallness. The Self itself might share in the ill luck of all its fellows. If for the individual every Tu or every Ille could become another Ego, the result, though intricate and confusing, might be desirable, but if the Ego simply resolved itself into another Tu or Ille — an odd case of that parity by reduction of which so much was lately heard in naval circles — the situation might tend equally toward the inefficient and the ridiculous.

The Self instructs us — with perfect thoroughness and without the faintest difficulty in the significance of a single plot or span of consciousness; after that, the transfer of this significance to other plots is a matter of imagination and analogy. If disinterestedness is the revealer of that equality in human values which is one indefeasible aspect of the facts, self-love is the revealer of that intensity in the same values which is another equally pointed aspect of the facts. The two facts, in combination, almost constitute a summary of life. Wisdom will derive its increments from both. Many a selfish man pities hunger, and he remembers others in his repletion partly because he forgot them altogether in his fast. The worth of a square meal may be the invaluable bridge by which a man passes from the idea of worth in himself to the idea of worth in his neighbor. Plainly, to crush or check egotism at a point short of that in which it is prepared to halve its accumulations with distinterestedness would not contribute finally to the enrichment or well-being of the latter. A wagon must be loaded before it can unload, and charity no less than luxury is an offspring and dependency of income. Men have sometimes enjoined upon others a contempt for Self, as they have similarly enjoined a contempt for sex, in the unconfessed prevision that the qualifications which they were careful to delete would be reinserted in the text by human nature. This may have been politic, but it was not philosophical. It is highly probable that the most disinterested of philosophers if commissioned by Providence to found and constitute a planet would not seriously consider the proposition of making everybody on the planet initially and unreservedly unselfish. "All for each and each for all" is an excellent motto; but it does not disprove, rather it implies and demonstrates, the thesis that our world is, basically, a world of *eaches*. No doubt men, like sexes, were divided that they might come together, but wisdom indorses both the separation and the rendezvous.

The Sermon on the Mount is thought to be the most visionary and least practical of sermons, yet it finds a basis in the Self for all its incitements to unselfishness. Here are precepts paired with motives. "Blessed are the poor in spirit: for theirs is the kingdom of heaven." "Blessed are the meek: for they shall inherit the earth." "Blessed are the pure in heart: for they shall see God." "Blessed are ye, when men shall revile you, and persecute you, and shall say all manner of evil against you falsely, for my sake. Rejoice, and be exceeding glad: for great is your reward in heaven." What would the author of these verses have replied to the suggestion that they should be revised on a basis of unmingled altruism? Emend as follows: "Blessed are the poor in spirit: for they have trampled on no man." "Blessed are the meek: for they have wrought evil to none." "Blessed are the pure in heart: for they have left the world unspotted." "Blessed are ye, when men shall revile you, and persecute you, and shall say all manner of evil against you falsely, for my sake. Rejoice, and be exceeding glad: for you have done no evil to your enemies." The Sermon on the Mount, which is so often criticized for extravagance, did not go all the way. It did not place its own exalted doctrine on a purely rational basis, the basis of what an enlightened and impartial spirit, disencumbered of the distracting prejudice of Self, would desire. It unabashedly points to benefits which in some future age or world will reward the farseeing Self for its sacrifices.

Few of us can now believe in the reality of these lofty and remote inducements. The Sermon on the Mount, therefore, breaks down; or, more exactly, its reasons break down. Its precepts are stronger than its reasons, but the impulse that led it to seek for these perishable reasons was an impulse which our better grounded sense will sanction. The lowest relevant fact cannot be left out of the most exalted calculations, and it is as impossible to ask the possessors of Selves to behave like selfless entities as it is to ask the possessors of bodies to behave as if they were disembodied spirits. Where society has based its organization on the principle of equal rights and equal benefits to all, the problem is already solved; the Ego and the Non-Ego feed amicably from the same trencher. These fields are extensive, yet restricted; and altruism probably cannot employ itself more usefully than in enlarging the territory within which altruism, in the sacrificial sense, is not demanded. There remain, however, and there will remain for a long time, outlying regions where the goods of the earth are distributed by competition or by conflict, where even the just and honest man has often to choose between his neighbor's welfare and his own.

It is easy to say in such cases "Choose your neighbor's"; but not only is it impossible to obtain general obedience for so hardy a precept, but it is doubtful whether, at the present stage of evolution, general obedience to such a precept would be beneficial. The Self is undoubtedly a power, and should be exercised; it is, at the same time, a menace, and should be disciplined. We cannot afford to have it stimulated into lawlessness; as little can we afford to have it chastened into imbecility. Possibly the best solution of this twofold necessity would be the establishment of two fields in one of which the Self should pursue its own good through its contributions to the general welfare, while in the other, under the inevitable restraints of honesty and justice, it should seek its own goal by its own path. This would seem to correspond to the hovering state of evolution which seems to hesitate between its old instrument, self-seeking, and its new instrument, self-subdual, just as it is said in the ornithorhyncus to hesitate between the laying of eggs and the bringing forth of living offspring. Such an accommodation has no logical warrant; it is pure makeshift, simple armistice, in a battle which can end only in one of two things, in the world's admission that the Self is autocrat, or in the Self's admission that its value and the value of its fellows is the same; in other words, in the Self's abdication.

The topic is old, yet I do not think that the sheer, simple opposition of the two principles, their real exclusiveness in spite of the fact that in actuality they are knit together in all sorts of temporary and temporizing combinations, is generally understood by thinkers. The strength of egotism lies in its wholeness, in its *integrity,* as an etymologist would say, and wherever it is quite authoritative and quite unmixed, as in an infant or in many animals, its dignity and rightfulness are instantly conceded. It is not merely that they can be nothing else; they are none the worse for not being anything else. The true defense of egotism is its finality; the moment it hesitates, shuffles, or goes halves, it loses ground. If a man said that he had rather have all the rest of the human race die in agony than endure the pain of toothache for a second, we should suspect a touch of falsity, a savor of bravado or defiance, in the speech; but if he quietly thought it or, better still, felt it without the effort or the tribute of a thought, we should feel a certain splendor in his attitude. The Self as universe — there is a kind of majesty in the idea; the phrase is almost identical with certain forms of the idea of God. Mr. Shaw does not go so far as this when he allows Andrew Undershaft to say in *Major Barbara:*

I moralized and starved until one day I swore that I would be a full-fed free man at all costs — that nothing should stop me except a bullet, neither reason nor morals nor the lives of other men. I said, " Thou shalt starve ere I starve"; and with that word I became free and great.

This is not egotism in its instinctive purity; it is an egotism that has bethought itself, that acknowledges the scruples it discards, that pays to its adversary the homage of defiance. Even so it breathes — as we remorsefully and tremblingly acknowledge — a harsh north wind of sanity. When egotism is unreserved, it dignifies even the contemptible. Hedda Gabler is a case in point. She is not only evil, but she is little and tawdry and vacuous; and yet she is, in a way, great and fascinating, because it has never occurred to her that significance could exist outside herself. As is shown clearly enough in the careers of the Tamerlaines, the

Alexanders, and the Bonapartes, the natural instinct, even the logical destiny of the Ego, is to make the globe its property and the race its slave.

Consistency on this line has its impressiveness, but consistency is never really possible. The moment a man admits that any other man authentically lives, he has put his foot upon a slope — acclivity or declivity, as disinterestedness or egoism pleases — on which there is no logical stopping place until the higher or the lower terminal is reached. If one other man is alive, all the rest are; if one man is alive at all, he is presumably as much alive as I. Practical stopping places there must be, and are; recessions even will occur: Nature sides with the Ego, whose parent she is, and Nature will apply the brakes to logic. If the Ego is bribed or scared into the service of its fellows, service will end at the point where the bribes and menaces expire. But the moment sensibility in another creature — sensibility *as such* — takes its place among values, among facts to be reckoned with, stability, consistency, is impossible, till a point is reached where every unit of sensibility anywhere is treated as of equal force with every other unit. Before we can fully grasp this fact, the understanding must perceive, and the imagination must realize, and the backwardness and stagnancy of these faculties will postpone for ages or cycles the grasp of the inevitable conclusion. Precept, ordinance, authority must be controlled in part by this immaturity or insufficiency of perception. It is one thing to perceive that the expedient conduct for a blind man and a seeing man in crossing a thoroughfare is precisely the same, and quite another to give advice to blindness on the supposition that one is addressing vision. Blindness limits possibility, and possibility governs precept.

Against this we must place the undeniable fact already pointed out that half the institutions in our democratic world are governed by this curiously practical idea that equal amounts of human sensibility are equally valuable without reference to distribution. All that we have to do is to transfer the principle from our institutions to our understandings, and to apply it at the same time to those parts of society where its validity still waits for public recognition. The Sermon on the Mount, in its own fashion, grasped the principle, and, in that aspect and to that degree, it is for the present age not so much a discarded superstition as an unattained and even, for the greater number of us, an unacknowledged, goal.

THE QUESTION OF DECENCY

THE question of decency is always to the fore in our time, and decency is believed by the decent to be eminently and profoundly reasonable. The odd thing is that they never furnish the reasons; they do not know the reasons; they cannot tell you, and do not wish to tell you, why decency should be, or why the line between the decent and the indecent should be drawn precisely where their age and race has willed to draw it. The mayor of New York told the great theatrical producers recently that something must be done to check indecency. Now it is extremely improbable that the mayor had ever asked himself if indecency be harmful, or why it is harmful; these are questions which the decent man thinks it almost indecent to put. The haters of war have reasons; the haters of drink have reasons; the haters of crime in sex itself have reasons: but the haters of indecency have none.

Much the same thing may be said of the lovers of indecency. Artists, it is true, claim that art in certain fields demands indecency, and scientists have been known to claim that truth in other fields requires indecency. These are reasons, sound or unsound; but they are pleas for indulgence to specialists; they do not assail general decency in the social order. In a wider view, the practicers of indecency never deny, or wish to deny, the position that abstract or general decency is useful. Indecency in their eyes is not a desirable and salutary custom; it is an agreeable and lucrative naughtiness. Their own debt to decency is enormous. Were indecency universal, there would be no salt — and therefore no cash — in its exhibition.

The battle between indecency and decency becomes, accordingly, a battle not of reasons but of assumptions, the assumptions that decency is necessary and that it is not. Since assumptions are highly militant, even more militant perhaps than reasons, the contest is enlivening and keen. We have, however, not a debate, but a quarrel. Why not turn it into a debate? Why not ask these people — both sides — what indecency will do or will not do to society? If either or both can tell us, that will be helpful; if neither can tell us, that will be interesting.

I have, in common with most educated men, a strong recoil from certain forms of indecency. The feeling has a warmth, a vigor, a momentum, which makes me feel that it ought to be utilized for the social good. It should defend, sustain, something. But what? In other men the same warmth is excited by other causes or other quantities of the same cause. I sit in the theater at an equivocal play between two men. My right-hand neighbor is tranquil before exhibits which shock me. My left-hand neighbor is shocked by things which leave me tranquil. Oddly enough, I despise both the tranquillity and the shock which I do not share; I call the one brutal and the other prudish. I despise my own feeling in another man when the provocation is different, though I am humane enough to be sorry for a man who is chilly in a room that I find warm. I despise my own feeling in another sense. Twenty years ago I felt as my left-hand neighbor now feels; twenty years hence I may be feeling with my right-hand neighbor. Plainly, here are three stages, three steps on a stair. Now a stair is a means of passage, is, in its very essence, transitional; and a step on a stair is the very last place that one can connect with the absolute or definitive in location. The top or the bottom, if reachable, would seem to offer better hopes of permanence.

Decency, then, is a variable between men and between states. It is likewise a movable in the same man and the same state. In America today we need no proofs of this; the atmosphere reeks with proof. Almost any practice may become the subject of a taboo, and a shock is producible by the violation of any taboo whatever. The feelings of insulted decency are as adjustable as they are strong, and this very power of adjustment leads us to doubt if their relations with their objects are either basic or abiding. This is confirmed by the observation that a large part of this recoil is panic, and panic, even when generally justified, is often quite in error as to the specific grounds for fear. The world loves and fears sex, and each man is chiefly afraid for his fellows, to whom he mentally transfers his own

fragilities without his own protections. Sex is a conflagration, yes; but is decency the fire engine which will
stop it, or is it merely the instinctive cry of "Fire"?
My own decency seems to me to be largely scare, and I
ask myself the question (which I have not yet answered): "Is the world's decency also scare, and does
scare avert peril?"

I speak of decency only, not of morality. Decency
is a part of manners; morality is a branch of conduct.
Decency differs from other manners in one curious
point. Other manners shut out the painful from human intercourse; decency (very largely) shuts out the
pleasant. A cynically sensuous line of Elizabethan narrative verse, "To hide those parts that men delight to
see," is perhaps the best brief illustration of the fact.
Of course the pleasure decides nothing. If the sight
of the pleasant is harmful, there is more reason to bar
it out than the sight of the unpleasant, which is merely
disagreeable. The point is that, if decency cannot stand
upon the ground of use, it will have some difficulty in
falling back upon the ground of pleasure.

This brings us to the crucial question: How far can
we prove that decency is useful? I can see just two
uses. It is clearly well that certain mutualities between
man and woman should be private, if only to prevent
interruption, and that the expulsion of organic waste
should be private in order that disgust may be confined to its originator. So far I can go; not a step further with any certainty or clearness. Even the second

of these points, the secrecy of disburdenment, amounts to little, since the race of its own free will keeps useful and even useless animals, whose offensiveness in this point is incorrigible. So far my reason goes with me; beyond lie custom, tradition, feeling, whether better or not than the opposite custom, tradition, feeling, I cannot say. I admit that a wide practice and a strong instinct create presumptions in their favor, but a presumption of exactly the same kind supports the chimerical belief in ghosts. Moreover, there are contrary presumptions which deserve a moment's notice.

Let the reader imagine himself as a primitive world-legislator, a Lycurgus whose Sparta is the planet. It occurs to him that a man should be allowed to expose his body and to reveal his mind in the exact degree that he sees fit. "Monstrous," you exclaim, "in the light of history and custom." Very well: look at it in advance of history and custom. How does it look? Does it not seem simple, natural, and reasonable, more than that, even — strikingly simple, natural, and reasonable? It falls in with the accepted and valid conception of liberty, that a man may do anything that does not bar his neighbor from doing just as much. If it be said that the neighbor has a right to protection from unpleasant sights, it might be bluntly retorted that the neighbor's eyelids, to say nothing of his back, might solve that difficulty. Or, if this be thought an impertinence, let us remind the objector that these are early days, and that the bans and stigmas

that are to make these objects painful sleep harmless
in the unconjectured womb of time. This proves nothing; it is mere presumption: but it seems to me as
strong — in other words, as reasonable — as the presumption which it contravenes.

It may be said that the sight of objects of desire
enkindles appetite. Sometimes, no doubt, but even
the gluttons seem to have no difficulty in passing fruit
stalls. The abundance is the safeguard. Nobody can
stop at all the fruit stalls, and the resistance, becoming
necessary, becomes habitual. Is it not clear that the
same result would follow the same abundance in the
offer to the eyes of the specific instruments of sex?
No man — not even Augustus of Saxony — could respond to all the solicitations; habits of rejection would
become inevitable; and choice would be shaped, as, on
the bodily plane, it is now shaped, by superiorities in
face and figure.

The words "face" and "figure" remind us of another obstacle to the discovery of a ground for decency
in reason. If desire were wicked, and decency were a
brake upon desire, its usefulness in that point would
be clear. But no one now believes the first of these
propositions, and the second is only a little less emphatically false. The enemy of desire is monasticism
or asceticism, not decency. If decency had this aim,
its first business would be to copy the harem in veiling
the face and to follow the convent in shrouding the
figure. But decency is no more hostile to desire than

table manners are opposed to appetite. Appetite sat on the commission that framed the manners. What both table manners and decency do is to prescribe a certain deliberation and tranquillity in the approach to the object of desire, and it is very interesting to note that table manners are able to reach this end without forbidding us to see or name the food. The difference between decency and indecency is not fundamental, like the difference between love and hate or wrong and right; it is rather like the difference between eating with one's fingers and eating with a knife and fork. Virtue is quite another matter; virtue protects us from unwholesome food. The contest between decency and indecency is the contest between two ways of reaching the same end, and that end is not the repression but the provocation of desire. By end I mean the end of the practice or institution as such; the ends of decent people are often very different and altogether higher. Decency and indecency angle for the same thing; only decency culls its baits. What do I say? Decency is itself a bait. "An inviting eye," said the kindly tempered Cassio, "and yet methinks right modest."

Deduction fails to find a ground for decency. What does induction — observation of men and peoples — say? At this point it is timely to repeat (that I may lessen a misunderstanding which no repetition can wholly avert) that I am not arguing against decency, or for or against any particular amount or kind of decency; my thesis is that we do not know, and that we ought to know, why we are decent. What, then, does observation show? That there is a comity or companionableness between the traits known as decency and virtue it would be foolish to deny. Nations relatively pure, the Germans of Tacitus, the Swiss, the Scotch, the early New Englanders, have almost always prescribed and practiced a strict decency. We are fairly sure that the virtuous people whom we know are decent, though we are not so sure that the decent people whom we know are virtuous. But we must not rush to the inference that the relation of decency to continence or purity is causal. Decency and purity are both forms of restraint, and the persons (or groups) to whom restraint is congenial are very likely to addict themselves to both. Decency and purity are both highly respectable, and the persons (or groups) to whom respectability is dear are prone to seek the countenance of both. This common affiliation with restraint and respectability might explain their companionship without establishing their consanguinity. Moreover, when a thing has a brand, and consequences follow, it is very hard to discriminate between the consequences of the brand and the consequences of the thing itself. Indecency is " low." Imagine it for a moment to be harmless and yet " low." What would happen? What would be left for the indecent person but low — actually low — society, low habits, low examples, in a word, demoralization? What we need, to prove the usefulness of decency, is a case in which a nation previously virtuous adopted and countenanced indecency — and lost its virtue. But what historian can point to such an instance? We need a History of Decency with express reference to its bearing upon virtue.

There are strange sentences in the ninth chapter of Westermarck's *History of Human Marriage.* "'Where all men go naked, as for instance, in New Holland,' says Forster, 'custom familiarizes them to each other's eyes as much as if they went wholly muffled up in garments.'" "It is not the feeling of shame that has provoked the covering, but the covering that has provoked the feeling of shame." In *The Isle of Penguins,* Book II, Chapter I, Anatole France is his own debonair self in the exposition of a similar philosophy. Combinations of indecency and virtue in individuals are not hard to discover either in history or in literature. Dean Swift is a case in point, perhaps Montaigne. Herodotus is as pure as he is frank, and that is saying much for his purity. "Plato," says Macaulay, "we have little doubt was a much better man than Sir George Etherege. But Plato has written things at which Sir George Etherege would have shuddered." Chaucer's Parson — the aggregate of perfections — said things that might almost have shocked Chaucer's Miller. Don Juan, on the other hand, seems to have been a very seemly fellow, seemly even in the unseemly Byron. The impulses to indulge and to restrain sex coexist in most persons, and the cheapest compromise for the libertine is to put his restraint into his manners and his licentiousness into his conduct. Immorality itself has its decency. There is decency in the entertainment, and also in the discarding, of a mistress. One remembers Lovelace's rather terrible remark that he made it a point to go to the funerals of all the women who died in childbed by him. King George the Second was trying to be decent when at his wife's deathbed he promised that thenceforth he would have only mistresses. In the same way decency has its immorality. Montaigne in the essay on Moderation gives at least two instances in which decency led men to the commission of evil.

Do history and observation make clear the need of decency? Not to me. But let us be generous (in these matters generosity is prudence). Let us suppose that the need is clear to other people. There remain two questions: What decency? and How much decency? to which the diversity of historical and contemporary practice can offer at the present time no reasonable answer. Our first task is to rationalize decency. What man knows why he is decent? I recoil with loathing from *The Captive,* but why? If some far-off sage or mage, some Plato or Zoroaster, were to say to me, not angrily or contentiously, but gently and ponderingly: "Do you *know* that harm would come if the world made it right for everyone to see such plays?" I could not honestly answer "Yes"; and the very persons who at this moment are throwing down this article in exasperated disgust would probe their minds to as little purpose in the search for a rational affirmative. I am not pleading for more or less decency; that is quite beside my point. I plead for a reasoned decency, more or less or what we have, as reason pleases. What humiliates me as a being who at least poses to himself as rational is to entertain violent indignation which I cannot justify, will not conquer, and do not silence.

If decency does good — any good — surely there must be some amount of decency, implying some definite barrier between decency and indecency, which is best for a given people at a given time. Why not work for the discovery of that amount instead of wasting our moral force on the defense of a position which is nothing more than an unreasoned, an unconfessed, and — what is still worse — a fluctuating compromise between tradition and impulse? We may fail? Certainly, but even the discovery that the whereabouts of decency was undiscoverable would be a powerful and needful aid in the determination of our moral attitude. If nobody can prove to us *that* Jerusalem is, or if nobody can show us *where* Jerusalem is, our attitude toward the crusade and its preachers must undergo a drastic transformation. The present movement toward outspokenness, painful as its extremes are to me and to others, ought at least to be a valuable experiment, but there is every prospect that its value will be wasted on our prejudice and ignorance. Suppose this movement met and crossed the ideal line between decency and indecency. It would cross that line without knowing it, as it would recross the same line without knowing it in the foreseeable reaction which, in another decade or two, will sweep us back along the road we have so hastily and inconsiderately traversed. The present movement can hardly last; it will be stopped. But it will not be worthily or wisely stopped; it will be stopped by an ascetic impulse, an impulse as blind, though not perhaps as low, as that which now furthers its advance, and the retreat which that impulse blindly dictates will be as meaningless and inconclusive as the march. Abject position for a civilized society — the position of a derelict ship, driven, now to north, now to south, by random, alternating blasts of irrational license and irrational stringency.

But is it not true that most reasonable people are decent, and that many decent people are reasonable? Yes; and it is an odd fact that decency is the matter on which reasonable people do not reason. This is largely explained by an unfortunate confusion between two battles which use in part the same field at the same time for their manoeuvers. The race as a race is over-sexed; sex must be disciplined; sex objects to discipline. This means a perennial battle, life-long in many individuals, age-long in every people, a righteous and a rational battle, because the evils which it opposes — I will name only two, prostitution and seduction — are practically undeniable and infect the marrow of society. Now this battle has been confused with another, the battle over the relatively superficial and external question as to how far a man should be allowed to expose his person and his thoughts to his fellow beings. On these points we have few rational data, and the combatants are instincts. What follows? The friends of righteousness become the friends of decency, largely because they believe that the enemies of decency are the enemies of righteousness. In this they are not far wrong. The motives for what is known at a given time and place as indecency are various, and are sometimes high. (One thinks of Thoreau with his sanative italics in "I care not how obscene my *words* are.") But, speaking generally, it *is* true that the indecency which confronts us in books and plays and spectacles, the indecency which makes our problem, emanates from persons who are on the wrong side in the conflict between right and wrong in sex. There is a base joy in sex, as there is a base love of gain which puts that joy to mercenary use. The extraction of *gold* from *dirt* was once a secret or subterranean undertaking; it is now transacted on the surface in the open. Now when people of this kind do things that we are not used to, we take fire, not so much because we mind the things as because we loathe the people. We defend the position that the enemy attacks less because we value the position than because we wish to whip the enemy.

Decencies, as we now hold them, are such positions. They are like barns or schoolhouses on battlefields that are given an accidental and transient value by the exigencies of a persisting conflict. If our own officers bade us give them up, the loss would not affect us keenly. Decent people would follow their own captains into indecency as coolly as some people follow their ministers into irreligion. But it is precisely these shifts that are the curious and compromising fact. We infer that things are wrong from the violence of our revolt, but, oddly enough, that very violence is fickle. Things that convulsed our fathers leave us calm. We absolve Whitman today for the things which we reprobated in the eighties, and we reprobate our contemporaries for audacities that are less pronounced than those of Whitman. The last thing that a *tradition* has the right to be is *capricious*. A tradition should know its own mind, or at least its own will.

Another curious fact about decency is that the indignations and the titillations go together. They are excited in different people, but they are excited by the same things. When the indignations move forward, the titillations keep them company. In general, that which cannot produce a virtuous horror will not arouse a guilty joy. The horror and joy both haunt the frontier that separates decency from indecency; that is the line of ferment, the line of excitability, the line of social gusto or disgust. The indignations and titillations are both borderers, the one trembling in the fear, the other panting in the hope, of forays. For this reason, no readjustments of the boundary which do not amount to the obliteration of all frontiers will ever rid us of indecency. When the *raided* parts are *ceded,* that is, when society says to indecency, "Speak out," they cease to be available for raids, and the cession neither concludes nor allays the conflict, which simply passes on to realign itself along the new frontier. Decency, likewise, is mainly interested in what it barely gets or barely fails to get. What fills its mind is not its Brandenburg but its Silesia.

The truth is that what perturbs the imagination is not so much the open or the plain per se as the unusual, and the unusual in concealment may affect the mind as powerfully as the unusual in exposure. The picture of an object when unexpected will produce commotions which the object itself in its familiar setting does not normally arouse, and so far does this curious process go that a thing so bodiless and fleeting as a name pronounced against expectation will move us more than the corresponding reality in its accustomed time and place. A debater's point might be made at this juncture by the suggestion that the same familiarity which has disarmed or sterilized the object might be equally efficacious on the picture or the name. But I care very little for *mere* debater's points, and I own to a doubt if either secrecy or exposure can help or hinder us very much in our personal and racial battles with the irrepressible suggestiveness of sex. Drapery is one expedient; disclosure is another: sex, up to a certain point, will circumvent either. Beyond that point, we must trust for our safety — such partial safety as can anywhere be found — to the health and virtue of the race.

In all this I have no wish to beg the question. If decency can help, let us take its help frankly and gladly, but first let it show us that its help is real. Decency is a screen — on that we are at one. The assumption that the screen is a bulwark is practically universal, so universal that it is practically never tested. Let it be tested. If the screen is all bulwark, keep it all; if it is half bulwark, keep the half; if it is all screen, away with it. The cost of that screen in time, in trouble, in self-restriction, in sacrifice, in hypocrisy, in shock, and in shame is very large: let us know what we are paying for. Let us put decency into one of three categories: the proved, the disproved, or the unprovable. Any one of the three dispositions would help. A reasoned decency, if obtainable, might hope to be relatively lasting. A migrating decency, an itinerant decency, such as we have had in America for the last thirty years, is a plain evil; it means two or three standards at once with two or three times the needful total of embarrassments and misunderstandings. Better a few undesirable licenses, better a few unnecessary restrictions, with *stability*, than a decency that is always of two minds about itself.

In some respects the present moment favors the establishment of that stability. One great historical ground for decency has been the chasm between age and age and sex and sex, the difference in knowledge between old and young and the difference in experience between men and women. The first of these intervals persists, though it is not so wide; the second may be said almost to have disappeared. Apart from the stubborn matter of physique, there is now practically but one sex, and everybody knows how effectually the reduction of the company to one sex simplifies the problem of decency. In late years, when the relation between the sexes has been unstable, the decency which is a consequence of that relation has been unstable, too. Equality in that relation is now achieved, with a prospect of at least provisional stability. Man—for the time being—will accept nothing less than equality; woman—for the time being—will demand nothing more. A decency formed today might have a chance of reasonable permanence—on one fixed condition, that it be a rationalized decency.

POETRY AND PROSE IN LIFE
AND ART

❧❧❧❧❧❧❧❧❧❧❧❧❧❧❧❧❧❧❧❧❧❧❧❧❧❧❧

In climbing a mountain peak we may feel at once sublimity and hunger: the same gasp expresses our wonder and our shortened breath. Reunions and partings, among the highest and tenderest passages of life, are associated with the cabman, the shawl-straps, and the luggage check. Birth and death, the altitudes of life, are encircled with displeasing and mechanical concomitants. The little, the dull, the sordid, the vulgar, have the impertinence and the ubiquity of flies: there is no thought, no man, no occasion, august enough to be secure from their intrusion.

It is apparent on a moment's thought that the poetry in life is inwoven with its other contents. To divide the poetry and the prose of life we should have to separate not day from day and hour from hour but moment from moment: nay, we should often halve the moment if our sifting were complete. The poetry and prose of life constitute not a bundle but a mixture.

It is admitted on all hands that poetical matter is but a small part of real or imaginable life, in other words, that the bulk of what we meet in experience, in records of experience, or in fictitious works is unpoetical.

The abundance of unpoetical matter and its intimate commixture with its opposite give rise to the problem of extraction. In many cases this is not a task. Artists are quick to discern and, where choice is free, to liberate available and beautiful material. Separations of this type are mere extensions of the work of instinct. A man may be conscious at the same time of awe and perspiration, yet if he be a man and not a churl, he instantly dissolves this chance alliance, claps the two feelings into distinct wards of his intelligence, and lays them up for separate revision. As long as literature merely follows this lead its selections are rational and healthy. Indeed, the being of poetry depends on its free exercise of this decisive privilege. If the power to select be withheld or curtailed, the other two facts, the extent of unpoetical material and the closeness of the intermixture, supervene with overpowering force to defile and abase the poetry.

The object of narration is to show that a series of particular events agrees with another series of general possibilities. We know that this *should* precede that in all cases; we see that this *does* precede that in the given case; it is the office of narrative to explain the event, that is, to prove this conformity. A narrator's first duty is to supply all, to forego nothing, that would show the actual series to be normal. The poet's first duty is to reject all matter that is not beautiful. The prescriptions of narrative are absolute, the interdicts of poetry are absolute. Will a conflict arise between these interdicts and these prescriptions?

If the tie of a kind conformed to the tie of cause, if the high and the mean produced each its own likeness as in the animal world the eagle and the snake begets each its own kind, there would be no jar between narration and poetry. Life, however, revels in the colligations of disparities. The coarse is linked with the delicate, the material with the ideal, the trifling with the momentous: the guano feeds the lily, the pickaxe uncovers the statue, the cackle of geese saves a citadel and a kingdom. Great deeds, delicate arts, demand as their condition the pursuit of petty and undignified details. The laws of cause and effect intersect the grades of dignity and excellence as the isotherms — to reapply an old figure — intersect the parallels.

Discrepancy and contradiction follow, the genius of narration, conformity to logic, finds itself at odds with the genius of poetry, fidelity to beauty. The poetical narrator is drawn two ways by two equally strong and equally authoritative forces. What as a narrator he is bound to seek he is bound as a poet to eschew. No shuffling, no subterfuge, can remove the hardships and mischiefs to which this strife of duties and demands subjects him.

The above conclusions apply mainly to long narratives. Life in bits is often homogeneous, and narration brief enough to utilize this uniformity; a ballad, for example, may escape the worst perplexities.

To be poetical, therefore, a narrator must often be obscure or incomplete; but this does not exhaust his difficulties. He is often bound to forego a large part of the interest and value of his subject.

Matter unavailable for poetry may be classified in five divisions:

First, the repulsive, comprising the rude, the clumsy, the grotesque, the coarse, the foul, the brutal, the ugly, and the rank.

Second, the arid, comprising the plain, the homely, the dull, the mean, the trivial, and also (through the common trait of incapacity to waken the imagination) the technical, the general, and the abstract. By way of the trivial the second class conducts us to the third.

Third, the humorous.

Fourth, the utilitarian, comprising the industrial, the economic, the commercial, the legal, and the political.

Fifth, the conventional, comprising usages which have become disjoined from feeling.

The contents of this list are large and rich. Three-fourths perhaps of all that men observe and study lies outside of the poetical demesne. It is clear that the poet must resign these springs of interest, and that it behooves him to consider when and for what it is worth his while to make the sacrifice. In life itself there is rotation in the exercise of faculties. Judgment, observation, conscience, sympathy, imagination, each is summoned in its turn, and the turn of each is short. I doubt if life yields ten minutes of unmixed poetical sensation.

If a man should suppress for one day every faculty except the imagination, half the profit of that day would be extinguished. If he viewed any long train of events through the medium of the imagination only, those events would undergo a like reduction: yet this is just what occurs in long poetical narrations. Selection is judicious when it finds its pattern in our instincts. If sensations of discrepant kinds assail the mind at once, the mind accepts the strongest or the sweetest and dismisses or neglects the others. It preserves its unity: it averts dismemberment. But it does not try to prolong this dictatorship: it calls up each faculty in turn to meet the fluctuations of experience. Experience shifts its quality many times in an hour, many times it may be in a minute. To refer all experience, to refer any large segment of experience, to the action of a single faculty would be a trial and a loss.

Let us dwell a moment on the case of humor. We have in humor a very special way of judging things, and a way which, in the measure of its specialty, is unfit for general or constant use. Humor, therefore, takes life in detail, not in sequence: its products are usually short or, as in *Don Quixote* and *Pickwick Papers,* consist of separate episodes. Comedy, which is long, is partly serious; and the farce, which is all humor, is unvaryingly short. The same principle applies to the imagination. The attempt to view the breadth of life through the slit of a single faculty is a double wrong — a wrong to the matter, half of which would be maltreated or expunged, and a wrong to the faculty, through its contest with intractable materials.

The thought advanced by Poe in his striking essay on the Tales of Hawthorne deserves to be adduced. He contends that a long poem is a contradiction in terms, because feeling can be maintained only for brief periods at the level requisite for poetry. It is undoubtedly true that successive exercise allows the powers of the mind to relieve and thus to refresh and renovate each other. The cause of beauty itself is served by an alternation which permits the esthetic faculty to repose and repair itself at the times of its displacement: nothing is so adverse to beauty as continuance.

The point has now been reached when the implication which has underlain our work thus far may be set forth in explicit words. Leaving the drama for the moment out of the question we may phrase our dictum thus: poetry is intense, select, exclusive; the lyric is intense, select, exclusive: the lyric is the proper form for poetry. Narration is diffusive, eclectic, versatile; prose is diffusive, eclectic, versatile: narration is appropriate to prose.

Prose is flexible and universal: it is suited to all subjects, all occasions, all degrees of emphasis. It is fit for prayer and jest, for dreams and recipes, for philosophy and gossip. There is no matter too large or too small, too high or too mean, to fall within its capacities and attributes. It is good enough for Milton in his picture of the nation roused from its sleep, and good enough for Ruskin in the poem to the Stones of Venice; yet it serves Mark Twain or Mr. Dooley with equal vigor and efficiency. Can we doubt that if life is to be set forth on a large scale the one instrument that fits the case is an instrument as versatile and manifold as life itself? One of the great utilities of prose is its aptness for discriminating emphasis. In all narratives, except anecdotes and fables, there are points that are both indispensable and trifling, points which we cannot omit and must not accentuate. We have to get our hero in and out of the room, to get him clad and unclad, to specify his route and his equipment, to explain his cousinship with the golden-haired and silken-vested damsel. Prose has a knack of doing all these things, of doing them efficiently yet lightly and without ado or bustle. Poetry can utter nothing that is not emphatic. To set off a thought in an isolated line is alone enough to give it emphasis, and when, over and above this, it is bedecked with rhythm, it has no longer any shelter for its insignificance. A mere detail, a foolish particular, which prose would push aside in half a dozen unregarded words, is doomed in poetry to distressing and unseemly prominence. A narrative poem is like an actor on the stage; it cannot shift its leg or raise its hand or crook its eyebrow without an anxious estimate of the effects of conspicuity. The drama, like narrative, has its necessary trifles; indeed, it is overstocked and cumbered with them; but a happy incident of its structure relieves it from the burden of expressing them in poetry. They are framed in prose and are known as stage directions. A narrative poet must insert his exits and his entrances in the very woof and substance of his poetry. If the authors of the Book of Common Prayer had sought to write the rubric in the style of the prayers and exhortations they would have met with similar perplexities.

We have set forth the difficulties that beset poetical narration. It will be interesting to observe the experience through which poets have sought an issue from those difficulties. It is plain that there are two courses, one of which or both of which the poet must adopt in cases of conflict. The poetry may succumb to the narrative, or the narrative may yield to the poetry: it is also possible that both may make concessions. It is clear that the choice will depend on the comparative weight which the poet assigns to his two functions of telling stories and purveying beauty. In early ages, when the story is the object and the beauty is the adjunct, it is evident that beauty must give way; in refined and cultured periods, when poetry is the end and the story is the vehicle, the narration will oftenest succumb.

It is found accordingly that the first expedient has been the usual if not the only resort of unlettered primitive ages, of the old, simple, historical, symbolical, and in many instances composite epics. In the *Beowulf,* in the *Nibelungenlied,* in the *Kalevala,* in the *Iliad,* the story is to the poetry what Rachel was to Leah. The singer's object is to get a narrative, clear, whole, and large, before minds not yet awake to standards and degrees of beauty. He presents without scruple and without shame whatever is related to the purpose. Here is a stanza from the *Nibelungen:*

Werbel as well as Swemline, the minstrels of the king,
To them no little profit did this fair marriage bring.
They gain'd, I ween, in largess a thousand marks or more,
When Kriemhild fair with Etzel the crown imperial wore.

(Nibelungenlied, Twenty-second Adventure,
Stanza XXXIX, Lettson's translation)

Here is also a passage from Homer:

He spake, Patroclus hearkened and obeyed
His well-beloved friend, who meantime placed
A block beside the fire, and on it laid
Chines of a sheep and of a fatling goat,
And of a sow, the fattest of her kind.
Automedon stood by and held them fast;
Achilles took the knife and skillfully
Carved them in portions, and transfixed the parts
With spits.

(Iliad, Book IX, 1: 252–260, Bryant's translation)

I refer the reader who is curious for more examples to the ninth canto of *Beowulf,* lines 1920–1935, and to the eleventh rune of the *Kalevala,* the speech beginning: "Vainly are your praises lavished" *(Volume I, p. 144, Crawford's translation).*

It is plain that we here find ourselves with a set of men who write narration always and poetry when they can; men to whom no doubt the adoption of rhythm did not mean a pledge of continuous beauty, but merely compliance with a rooted usage. Their works are not poems in the proper sense: they are compilations of poetry and prose. The injury is great, but one cannot but feel that the honest and simple hardihood of these upright and plain-spoken persons is far ahead of the shambling modern trick of shuffling and evasion. Beauty wanders in and out of the Homeric epic as it wanders in and out of life itself; its approach is always welcome, but no attempt is made to arrest or to conceal its departure. We know that it is real because it comes and goes; if it stayed we should begin to question its reality. It must be remembered also that the effect of pettiness and incongruity is greatly modified by the removal of the action to an ancient time and by its exposition in a foreign language. It was a great help for Homer that he could say " tunic " instead of " shirt " and another help that he could say " chiton " instead of " tunic." Homer can let us safely into Agamemnon's tiring chamber; but make the poet, the monarch, and the garment English, and one shudders at the risk of the experiment.

The practice of the early, instinctive epics has not been usual in modern times, but it has found disciples in vigorous, daring, and eclectic minds who saw much that was strong and unpoetical and who could keep back nothing that they saw. But the practice in our days is infelicitous; it has to reckon with a sterner standard and a finer taste. Walter Scott is not ashamed of lines like these:

No summons calls them to the tower,
To spend the hospitable hour.
To Scotland's camp the Lord was gone;
His cautious dame, in bower alone,
Dreaded her castle to unclose,
So late, to unknown friends or foes.

This is honest certainly; there is no subterfuge or glozing in these frankly and oppressively prosaic lines; but we feel inclined to put to the verses the question of the Hebrew parable: "How camest thou in hither having on a wedding garment?" The fault here is not so much in the suiting of plain words to plain thoughts — a practice which is sound and right — as in using rhythm where rhythm is not wanted nor in place. Matthew Arnold once compared Wordsworth's sorry attempts to lift a platitude with Homer's daring plainness in a like emergency. This is no doubt very sound; but if it is wrong to make your words gay when your thought is homely, is it not just as wrong to make your movement airy when your thought plods? In cases of this kind both rhythm and gay diction are bedizenments, and the plan of work which enjoins one and promotes the other is a plan that has an error at its root.

Walter Scott, however, is not the only sinner among recent poets. The two most impetuous and untrammeled poets of the last century, Robert and Elizabeth Browning, carry the practice to the height of extravagance and daring. They remove the barrier; they dismiss the sentry; they allow the whole wide, motley, jostling world of modern life to make an uncontested entrance into compositions which they cast in meter and publish in the guise of poems. In *Aurora Leigh* and *The Ring and the Book* nothing that prose would approve is rejected by poetry. It is hardly needful to remind the reader of the church gossip in *Aurora Leigh* at the time of Romney's contemplated marriage or of the pleas of the rival advocates in *The Ring and the Book*. I do not mean, of course, that poetical beauty is absent in either poem or is uncommon in *Aurora Leigh*. But it is hard to measure the disturbance, the distraction, and the chaos which the letting down of every bar, the indorsement of any subject or any word, has induced in these remarkable productions. Things that in themselves are sound and worthy, that are in essence strong, brilliant, vivid, or acute, are turned into blemishes and sins through the mere circumstance that the narrative is cast in poetry.

We have seen the effects of catholicity and license; let us now view the results of exclusion and reserve.

In modern times a man is usually a poet first and a narrator afterward; and he is apt to feel keenly his poetical obligations. He is bound or feels that he is bound to be continuously beautiful, and his narrative must bend or seem to bend to this cardinal and paramount requirement. He has too much taste or too little courage to adopt the early plan of being plain where truth is plain: he is pledged to constant beauty, and he must plot and shuffle to make good his pledge. If he chances to be averse to homeliness and tolerant of insincerity he will write as Pope or one of Pope's lackeys writes in the rendering of the first book of the *Odyssey:*

> The golden ew'r a maid obsequious brings,
> Replenished from the cool, translucent springs;
> With copious water the bright vase supplies
> A silver laver of capacious size.
> *(Odyssey, Book I, 1: 179–182, Pope's translation)*

This is of course a cheap veneer, a patent and obtrusive falsity. But a veneer not quite so cheap, a falsity not quite so patent, is imposed on every long narrative poem that aims to be strict in its loyalty to beauty. In *The Castle of Indolence,* in *Lamia,* in *The Revolt of Islam,* in *Lalla Rookh,* in *The Excursion,* in *Evangeline,* in *The Idylls of the King,* in *The Earthly Paradise,* the same error incurs the same penalty. We have here the old struggle of the narrow and special form with the broad and general material. The attempt to sleek over or the resolve to cast out whatsoever is common or unclean impairs the truth of the whole poem as well as of the single passage; it diffuses insincerity, and destroys the force of beauty by the abstraction of the element of contrast. Nothing shows the difference between poetical and prose narration more distinctly than the *Morte d'Arthur* of Sir Thomas Malory and *The Idylls of the King,* its latest and most brilliant paraphrase. The *Morte d'Arthur* is nearly — it is only through fear of the public that I forbear to say quite —

as poetical as the *Idylls;* and in variety, in ease, in pliancy, in freedom, and in truth it is hard to be just to the extent of its superiority. In Malory the plain and ugly things are usually right: in Tennyson the beautiful and finished things are often wrong. Even Tennyson, though a careful, is not a squeamish writer. He takes us with Gareth into the court kitchen, and tells in "The Last Tournament" how a damsel, finding the wine unsavory, "spat and pished." I do not wish to impugn this phrase, but rather to suggest the tact and art involved in the reconcilement of such phrases with the needs of poetry, and the failure of the utmost art and tact to make them otherwise than disagreeable. What soundness can there be in a literary form which cannot say what it is bound to say without a stratagem, and which makes it an offense to utter what it would be a blunder to omit?

Out of these difficulties emerges a corrective practice which operates at once as a relief and a distemper. The modern narrative poet, alive to the dinginess and dullness which nearness and intimacy have imposed on the contemporary setting, reverts to the past or to some unknown and far-off region where the charm and the indistinctness of distance may help him to ennoble his material. Almost all epics, almost all narrative poems, of our time are set in a remote and often in a dim and legendary epoch. Antiquity is their retreat and hiding place. Undoubtedly there is some help in this reversion, but the price of the relief is onerous. We can lessen the effect of a mole or pimple on a lovely face by removing it to a protective distance, but the effect of every charm is correspondingly attenuated. The location of an epic in a far-off and unsubstantial period of time deadens alike the vividness of its prosaic and its poetical components. If Tennyson assigns his romance to Camelot instead of Liverpool he has escaped the cross of reckoning with street cars, water pipes, and costermongers, but he has to face the other far from trifling difficulty of his total ignorance of life in Camelot. We touch here upon a further ground for the unreality and emptiness of modern epics. If anyone will compare *Hermann und Dorothea,* in which poetry means little more than the punctual recurrence of hexameters, with poems like *Lamia* or *Jason,* he will understand the width and force of this restriction.

We have now reviewed the two expedients for the adjustment of narrative and poetry, and we have seen that the evils of license and the evils of restraint are alike stringent. In these cases there is no right course. It is wrong except for contrast to admit bald or flat or trifling passages into works of which every line is understood to be poetical; and it is wrong to hide roughness with veneer. Both beauty and sincerity are imperative in poetry, and a form in which each excludes the other is unsuited for poetical designs.

At this point a question may present itself. The drama is in its essence a long narrative; it is often poetical; does it then fall under the drawbacks of poetical narration? If we are not ready to proscribe the drama with the epic, are we not forced to indorse the epic with the drama? Let us see what answer can be found to this suggestion.

First of all, the drama has receptacles or pockets, cast in prose and known as stage directions, which relieve its verse of a good part of its unavailable and hampering material. The length of the drama, moreover, is cut short by the brevity of stage performances. Again, there is much to raise the level of dramatic matter. Passion is large and high, and the drama is the vehicle of passion. The drama, on its poetical side, consists of human speech, and human speech, in strong and stirring situations, has the select, intense, exclusive quality which is suited to the ends of poetry. The drama suffers less than an epic from a meddlesome and hampering environment. All these points, though weighty, are subordinate: the great difference between the narrative poem and the poetical drama is that in the first narrative is a form which poetry takes and in the second poetry is a form which drama takes. Poetry is the first thing in an epic, the second thing in a drama. As we listen in the theater or read in the closet, the truth or falsity of the feeling and the action diverts our minds from estimates of beauty. So true is this that we speak of the poetry in a drama, in *Romeo and Juliet* or *A Midsummer Night's Dream,* for instance, as something distinct from the body of the play and, still more oddly, the parts that we call poetry are very often undramatic. The even maintenance of beauty is by no means felt as a desideratum: we weary of the scenes in *Henry IV* or *Edward II* in which Shakespeare and Marlowe seem to seek this uniformity. The public attitude is evinced in a specialty of nomenclature. We speak of prose dramas and poetical dramas with readiness and confidence because we feel that poetry is secondary in dramatic work. But we do not, except by a rare license, speak of prose epics or of prose lyrics, because we feel that in lyrics and epics poetry is the supreme essential. A drama recast in prose remains a drama: an epic or a lyric would perish in the alteration. Shakespeare allowed himself to mix prose and verse in his dramatic work: why is it that no epic writer ever ventured on a corresponding liberty? Even when blank verse is retained it is often in dealing with prosaic matter divested of poetical suggestions. Blank verse may be used to strengthen, not to beautify. There is no more poetical beauty in Hotspur's story of the popinjay than there is in Goldsmith's picture of Beau Tibbs; but the rhythm is not useless or tawdry, for its object is to quicken and exhilarate.

We conclude, then, that poetry is suited to lyric and drama, that prose is the proper medium of narrative. No one of course would have the folly or the courage to deny that the world's best minds and best work are represented in poetical narration. Homer, Virgil, Dante, Spenser, Milton — these are no vulgar or petty names; but it will be found in nearly every case, I think, that it is the man who has saved and glorified the clumsy and unpleasing form. The *Iliad* is great rather as it is Homeric than as it is epical: the *Aeneid,* as Virgil, is priceless; as an epic it is but a mean affair. The *Faerie Queene* is all very well in so far as it is Edmund Spenser, but in so far as it is a narration in verse it is a tedious and lamentable blunder. Of the *Orlando Furioso* and the *Jerusalem Delivered* what can be said, even by those who are just to the cleverness of the one and the loftiness of the other, except that as wholes they are wearisome and futile? In the cases of Dante and of Milton it cannot be denied that the epic form has rendered one real, though narrow, service: it has granted that lofty and immeasurable vista which meets our reverted vision as we stand at the summit and conclusion of their works. But aside from this unique impression — an impression of brief extent and accessible only to the very few who read the works in course and who read them through — the epical form of *Paradise Lost* and the *Divine Comedy* is a burden and a weariness. There is little doubt that great epics are the least read and the least readable of all literary products of the first order. Successful narrative poetry becomes more and more difficult as time advances, nations mature, and the standard of poetical requirement attains a higher level and a firmer sway. More and more it becomes clear that the true and abiding forms of poetry are the lyric and the drama.

POETRY INSURGENT AND RESURGENT

HENRY JAMES, the beloved recreant, became an English citizen for the sake of the right to say "we" after a victory. Without copying his bold step or war-like motive, I shall use "we" in this essay to comprise both Englishmen and Americans, and what is said of the English applies largely, though not strictly or evenly, to my own countrymen.

Some weeks ago I remarked in conversation that the English tongue, like the English mind, in its daily use and wont, was unpoetical, and that this circumstance was a hardship and a drawback to our poetry. My friend observed that with Spanish, his mother tongue, this was not the case; Spanish in daily use is half poetry, even as certain voices, in common speech, are half music. In English two evils result: we have to go twice as far to get our poetry, and our poetry, when reached, is twice as far from our hearts, our habits, our simple ease and cheer. A dilemma ensues: either our verse, obedient to the ideals of poetry, maintains a high, un-broken level of ornament and distinction, at the cost of a troubling estrangement; or, obedient to the temper of the language, it achieves ease and fellowship at the price of marked inequalities, frequent descents, and a liberal inclusion of the rugged and commonplace.

POETRY INSURGENT AND RESURGENT

My thesis is that during the last two centuries English poetry has accepted a principle which is Spanish or Italian rather than English — the principle of uninterrupted beauty and distinction; that, while we still want poetry, we do not want that kind of poetry; and that the unrest, the discontent, and the revolt which have unsettled the poetical composition of the last fifty years are aimed at the replacement of English poetry on its primitive and rightful English basis. The law which governs our poetry today is the acquired and alien law of constancy in beauty with variations and inequalities in life; the ancient and native law for English verse is constancy in vitality with interruptions or disparities in charm.

The principle is not confined to Britain: it is the basis of primitive poetry everywhere; we may surmise that the Greeks, conforming to a like expectation, found in Homer a vivid and spirited novelist, in the *Iliad* a sublimated *Treasure Island,* in the *Odyssey* a glorified *Robinson Crusoe.* But the mark of the tendency is clear on our earlier and larger poets. Chaucer, with his ingratiating ease and his cheerful shedding of responsibility, flutters from grave to gay, from plainness to ornament, with the unconcern of a bird for whom the ownership of wings has made the world a plane. Shakespeare recalls his own Prince Hal in his adaptation to all levels. He can say in one place —

By heaven, methinks, it were an easy leap
To pluck bright honour from the pale-faced moon —

and, thirty lines further on, can talk in this fashion —

But that I think his father loves him not
And would be glad he met with some mischance,
I would have him poisoned with a pot of ale.

This is no shift from scene to scene or from mouth to mouth; it is the same mouth in the same scene, and the instance is not untypical either of Shakespeare or of his brother Elizabethans. Even Spenser, though a sumptuous and opulent writer, is the opposite of finical.

The evil began, I think, with Milton. That studious and meditative mind, in the bright seclusion of its youthful scholarship and the dark seclusion of its uncherished age, found leisure to perfect and mature its English until every word took on the potency and pregnancy that words possess in an oath or a spell. Later on, in the mid-eighteenth century, came those literary illuminators of missals, Collins and Gray. Then came that tender effulgence of the Georgian awakening, the dearest, though not the highest, moment in our literature, when English became for a few years almost a Romance tongue, and when, in Shelley and Keats at least, spontaneity became for once not the adversary but the associate and ally of the principle of undeviating beauty.

In this world the exquisite is the momentary. The shades of the prison house closed around that heaven in which the infancy of the nineteenth century had found a Wordsworthian cradle. And then came Tennyson, to whose diversity my concision is unjust— Tennyson the gifted, the regal, to whose magic and whose sovereignty we may perhaps largely refer the impasse in which English poetry at this crucial moment finds itself. He took up the work of Coleridge, Keats, and Shelley: of their outcry he made his ritual; of their impulse he made his law. The belt of style was tightened round the shapely figure of the gasping but submissive Muse. Matthew Arnold, a man of high poetical ideals, with which his practice occasionally caught up, wrote a verse which on the whole confirms the esthetic stringency of Tennyson. The tendency was prolonged, if not augmented, in the mingled nectar and narcotic of Rossetti, and in Swinburne's unearthly effect of league on league of dancing phosphorescence. How strongly the influence survives may be proved by a reference to such Americans as George Sterling, William Rose Benét, Brian Hooker, Alexander Percy, Grace Hazard Conkling, Olive Tilford Dargan, and Josephine Peabody Marks.

Meanwhile the race and its poetry drift apart. Books of verse find authors, publishers, critics; the reader alone is coy. This reluctance transcends the proletariat or bourgeoisie of letters; it attacks the educated, the cultivated, the lovers of beauty, the lovers of literature, in a sense, the lovers of poetry itself. I love poetry if the proneness of lines to burrow and nest in my memory be an index of that love; yet for my own will or weal I would not read one-twentieth, one-fiftieth, part of the matter which I consume in the penance of reviewership. I would not willingly read even the poetry that I respect and applaud. If this be set down to the peevishness of satiety, let me ask any reader if, in that baptism in Castaly with which no man of culture would dispense, he would not in all candor prefer sprinkling to immersion. The reason is not dark. The dean of American letters has hinted, in words which I paraphrase, that poetry is an interspersion, even an aspersion, in the normal life of man. Perusal means unbroken poetical sensation. Why should I, who doubt if actual living ever yielded me five minutes of unqualified and consecutive poetical experience, demand that sensation by the hour, when the vehicle is literature? For me poetry dots life; I could wish that it dotted literature also.

I cannot read poetry long with comfort unless it be mixed with other elements. I adapt myself to the Shakespearean drama, because Shakespeare, good fellow that he was and is, allows me so often to forget the poetry. But modern verse-drama is scantily read, in spite of the premium offered by the presence of a story in action. In this favored field, where drama might have expected to preside at the resurrection of poetry, poetry officiates at the interment of drama. "'Tis a very excellent piece of work," said that incisive judge of arts and letters, Christopher Sly; "would 'twere done." Even narrative poetry is respectfully forsaken. Our lads are unresponsive to Scott, and the poetic treasure of *Paradise Lost* is deposited in a safe of which posterity has mislaid the combination.

How far this incapacity is peculiar to our race, I have no leisure to discuss. It is not improbable that the intensity of our labor, the insalubrity of our climate, the opacity of our senses, the terrible omnipresence of that death-in-life which is known as organization, may have sapped our power of continuous receptivity. Nor shall I ask how far the defect is confined to our era. It seems probable enough that the vast expansion of business and of science, two forces which in their ripeness and complexity are churlish to that poetry with which their infancy was sociable, may have impaired a sensibility which brightened life for our ancestors. It is probably true, as Lowell suggested, that the language has lost its docility to the tutelage of verse. Words lose their poetic values in daily speech, and the restoration of this forfeit virtue in the hour of demand becomes increasingly difficult. Types of English unfriendly to poetry leave their finger marks on the words that poetry must use — newspaper English with its resonant vacuity, technical English with the Libyan monotony of its waterless and featureless expanse, statutory English, the legal *sentence,* symbolic in its length and dreariness of that other object of the same name to which its contents so often warningly point. The outcome is natural enough; the poet is tempted to recast the refractory language, and in the recast it becomes a foreign tongue.

But even while the coil was tightening round poetry, protest and revolt could not be quieted. There is one not inconsiderable section of poetry, comprising the dialect poem, the humorous poem, the military poem, and the adventure poem, which has remained intractable to the esthetic yoke. This type, which reverts to the medieval ballads, if not to *Beowulf,* has been possibly the lustiest and healthiest section of English poetry since the departure of Shakespeare and the advent of Milton. "Horatius," of bridge-keeping fame, is neither so high nor so fine as "A Dream of Fair Women," but it is firmer pulsed and warmer blooded. "Danny Deever" is less refined but more racial than "Lamia" or "Isabella" or even the "Ode to Melancholy." The debt we owe to sheer dialect for the maintenance of robuster ideals of poetry is considerable. Burns was a loosening, if not a liberating, influence. The Muse, who had grown ladylike with Gray and Collins, in her scamperings over gorse and heather with Robert Burns put on freckles, which her resumption of veil and parasol in the ensuing century never quite removed from her expressive face.

The Biglow Papers, published in the crucial forties and sixties in our own country, proved the capacity of dialect to set forth lofty purpose and vigorous thought, and to skim lightly up and down the long scale that divides the grotesque from the sublime. That problem of rising, sinking, and rising again with ease, which is well-nigh insoluble for Miltonic and Tennysonian verse, is solved by dialect with curious deftness and dispatch. Dialect can entertain that rudeness which is often a half-virtue without falling into that cheapness which is universally a sin. Its part in poetry is that of an elevator in a building, which, keeping its headquarters in the basement, makes itself in succession contiguous to all levels. If it be asked why its universal adoption should not lead us out of all our difficulties, the answer is simply that the virtue of dialect is occasional; on becoming standard it would lose its freedom. You cannot keep house in an elevator.

Many things in our day have exalted the muscular and manly lyric, the lyric of furrow, shaft, and trench. There were Bret Harte's Californian narratives, to which Eugene Field's later experiments were related as treble to baritone; there were John Hay's few but widely read *Pike County Ballads;* there was the fiery onset of Mr. Kipling's troopers before which the routed public made way in unconditional surrender; and, still later, the thronging arrows that sang and glinted in Mr. Chesterton's battle-shaken verse. But, useful as these poems were in keeping alive the tradition of an un-shackled and adventurous poetry, they constituted merely an inclosure, a bounded plot of verse, subject to its peculiar customs. The freedom of their methods influenced the stricter poetry hardly more than the waiving of the dress suit in the entertainments of the Bronx impairs its obligation on Fifth Avenue. The higher and prouder verse had to reform itself from within, and I ask you to follow with me a few steps in its self-renovation.

The first place in the record belongs to Words-worth's plea, enforced by precept and example, for a poetic diction which should reflect the language of actual men when that language was swayed by emotion. The theory had its infirmities, and Wordsworth, in whom, as everybody knows, the genius and the prophet made common house with the simpleton and the prig, was clumsy both as exponent and as illustrator of its virtues. His specimens sometimes justified, more often caricatured, his theory, and new methods in his later poems impeached the soundness of his earlier doctrine. An enemy or satirist, wanting my own reverence for Wordsworth, might declare that the brayings of his ponderous and Latinized maturity were intended to drown out the bleatings of his youth. I content myself with the remark that his retreat had all the poignancy of retractation.

Wordsworth, with his great name and sound intent, accomplished little for the cause; far more was achieved by the headstrong impulse of that dauntless gladiator, Robert Browning. The service did not come from the eccentric and acrobatic Browning, and it found no sustenance in his crabbedness, his obscurities, his verbosities, and his circumlocutions. It was the sane and normal Browning, the Browning of "My Last Duchess" and "Andrea del Sarto," who served us stoutly by the demonstration that poetry, without abandoning its final reserves of elevation and distinction, might be generously inclusive, both in the range of its topic and allusion and the varied graduation of its tone. This was true help, and simplified the problem.

The next person to be dealt with is Whitman. That curious being was a sort of Krishna—or perhaps only a Krishna Mulvaney—and the homage which one element of our public pays to his godship may be correlated with that devotion which a less lettered section offers on the shrine of Mrs. Eddy. Some injustice was done him in his lifetime, and a compunctious posterity has been increasingly liberal of expiations. In the conflict between himself and public opinion, Whitman incurred rather than achieved a victory, and we have complied with military usage by paying him indemnity ever since. In my judgment Whitman's positive contribution to the movement has been meager. No doubt his peculiarities and his reputation, acting in concert, have been negatively helpful in giving a powerful jolt or concussion to the old narrowly limited and stubbornly intrenched conception of poetry. But we must bear in mind that Whitman's innovations are referable less to the breakdown of the tradition before his powers and demands than to the breakdown of his capacities before the strength of its requirements. Whitman went barefoot, if the metaphor be forgivable, not from that conscientious and deliberate preference for bare feet which is the index of self-respecting boyhood in America, but because he could not get his foot into the shoe. He shirked meter, and the shirker cannot help us. I grant him scattered inspirations, but no competence; and no man can strike a new and lasting balance between inspiration and skill who is not at the same time skillful and inspired. Whitman's bulkiness, his prattle, his laxity, the piling up of formless lists, like family furniture in the mover's van (the least reputable and seemly objects in the ménage putting on a dismaying prominence in the portentous load), all these things are signs of an inaptness for leadership in a literary reform.

Thomas Hardy's recklessness in the support of freedom took half the value from his courage. A born artist, in a mood of recalcitrancy toward art, at the very moment that he vivified his poetry with energy and passion he allowed it to become almost churlish in its refusal of amenities. In our advanced epoch poetry admits rawnesses that careful prose would hardly tolerate, as advanced women listen composedly to utterances that are rather disconcerting to men. Hardy's verse repoints the lesson that poetry, in doffing the purple, need not and should not put on the wolfskin.

George Meredith, with his rich poetical endowment, his fearlessness, and his serene command of the impossible, might have seemed the destined renovator of our verse; but unluckily he outran the tradition in the very points of diction and ornament in which the tradition itself was peccant. By contrast with his remoteness our Tennysons and Rossettis grew neighborly and familiar, as a European impresses us like a compatriot when we meet him in the presence of an Asiatic.

Meredith, then, hardly figures in the return to Lebanon, and Hardy's aid is checkered if not dubious. A third Englishman, Mr. John Masefield, their fellow in scorn of convention and plenitude of temperament, outdid them in efficiency of service. I do not include in this service the violent and ribald diction which supplied his early narratives with a flaring advertisement for which he atoned in the double penalty of narrow blame and shallow praise. This was an incidental error. He was right in his perception that the specific for our poetic ills is the shift of emphasis from beauty to life — I would personally add without effacement of beauty — and a man of his origins must not be too roughly chidden if he put the headquarters of vitality in the barroom and the prize ring. He helped us by showing that the sorry and homely face of common life is to be ameliorated, not by the application of salves or unguents to the surface, but by the lighting up of its rude features through the infusion of new blood-warmth from the heart. I add in frankness that my approval of the tendency does not embrace all its illustrations.

To recross the Atlantic, two American poets, so unlike that their names are probably now coupled for the first time, have done strange and daring things with the most patrician of English measures — blank verse. They have stripped that august meter of its trappings and its trammels; they have warped and wrung its feet; they have replaced its ancient oratorio harmonies with a rude and hearty music not unrefreshing to the pampered ear; they have pared diction, in an emphatic sense, *to the quick,* and have shown how the language of poetry can largely recover, through passion, the dignity it has lost through homeliness. The first of the two men is our foremost academician, William Dean Howells, whose blank verse dialogues, like "The Father and Mother" and "The Mother," were offered to the half-reluctance of a drowsy public, incredulous of the possibility that a man who wrote placid verse in his twenties and thirties should make his seventies vibrant by original and moving poetry. The second is Mr. Robert Frost, a younger writer, with more drama and more incisiveness, who in his remarkable *North of Boston* undertook, not without success, the surgery of our inflated literature. In his later volume, *Mountain Interval,* he has sometimes reminded us that the surgeon is related to the executioner.

From *Spoon River,* on the other hand, with its institution of a post mortem on a civic scale, I think we draw no solid help. I do not complain of Mr. Masters for serving poetry to me in an earthen jug; my complaint is that in *Spoon River* at least, in pouring the precious liquid from the Venetian chalice into the earthen jug he has spilled the poetry. I would not deny to Mr. Masters the honor of enrollment in the great uprising which tends to renovate the conduct and the aims of poetry; and the free-verse people in general must be credited with enlistment, if not with achievement, in the cause. Their post on the battle front has been unhappily chosen. They are a sort of Rumania, cleaving to the right side, as sides go, in their late entrance into the enlarging conflict, but unwise in the choice of an antagonist, and likely to incur humiliations which may prove to be a stumblingblock to their allies.

While I would on no account deter any man from writing any kind of verse which he can make agreeable to other men, I do not think that meter has been a prime offender in the transactions which subject poetry to attack. The prime offenders are diction, tone, and subject. Meter in English is a good creature, a decent body, exempt from aristocratic predilections; the very existence of the word "doggerel" connotes its friendly openness to all kinds of homespun and hearty affiliations.

The career of free verse has been marked by a diverting irony. Adopted in France as the fine extremity of a long process of refined esthetic evolution, and transmitted with due solemnity to elect recipients in England and America, it was acclaimed in our simpleminded country as a release from artistic toil and a signal to expectant myriads. We hailed the tardy fulfillment of the biblical prediction: "Then shall the lame man [the man limping in his prosodic feet] leap as an hart, and the tongue of the dumb sing." Everyone could now write verse, and Parnassus was safe for democracy. We surpassed our redoubtable precursor, Molière's M. Jourdain, in the discovery that we had all been talking *poetry* all our lives.

I shall not linger on the various follies which grimace and chuckle on the edges of the particolored movement. In revolutionary or rebellious times the fools are perennially active; they want another chance. The leaders are of another class, and my main point is that even efforts which are puerile as outputs are respectable as symptoms. They afford an illustration of the reach and scope of the movement for the restoration of our displaced poetry to its proper basis.

Let me sum up the situation briefly. During the last two centuries a gap has arisen between the poetry that we want and need and the poetry that is supplied by our artists. The true English note in verse is heartiness, lustihood, marrow; the note of our recent poetry has been fineness, rarity, distinction. I would not say that our masters of finish have actually wanted life, but they have so far embosomed and secreted that life as to place it beyond instant and general reach. The watch has continued to tick, but the massiveness of the gold casing has made its beats barely audible to the quick ear. Now the return from cunning to nature is by no means infrequent in literature, but the movement was embarrassed in our case by the fact that the daily speech, perhaps the hourly thought, of a stock inherently poetic was leaning more and more toward the pedestrian. We found ourselves in the dilemma of a man obliged to choose between a costly and luxurious habit which cramped his breath and impeded his movements and a plain working-suit too homely to be

presentable. The public attitude bred a further compli-
cation. Reform could be final only when the changing
practice of poets was met halfway by the changing taste
of readers. A division had grown up between the *taste*
of the public and its *appetite,* and our tongues hankered
for piquancies which we felt to be innutritious to our
systems.

These points are aggravations of a problem which at
this hour is not fully solved or even assured of solution.
Its mere existence, however, testifies to the strength
and soundness of the enduring English instinct, and
imparts to the history of poetry in our day that dramatic vigor which its solution may hand on to the
poetry itself.

ACTION IN DRAMA: WHAT IT IS AND IS NOT

I SHOWED a manuscript play to the director of a theater. Between civilities he found time to remark, "No action. I keep waiting for somebody to get up and smash a window." I agreed with his doubts of the play; I agreed with his distrust of the action. Our point of difference was that I was perfectly calm on the absence of smashed windows.

This led me to ask myself what action was to a manager, to a playgoer; what it was to myself. The conclusions I reached seemed to me to be new, although this novelty may be simply the measure of my ignorance.

The average playgoer tends to think that speech and action are divided, though adjacent, fields, that they represent two degrees of vividness, and that action stands for the superior degree. When one man on the stage kills another, that is action; when he puts his feet upon a table, that is action. The actions differ greatly in importance (the playgoer sees that), but for him they possess in common an important something which is not possessed by the most passionate or energetic speech. A man robs a till—*Action*. A judge says "Three years"—*Speech*. A man boards a

steamer — *Action*. A sovereign's voice orders his fleet
to move against the enemy — *Speech*. A man writes a
challenge to a duel — *Action* (he uses his hand). He
utters a challenge to a duel — *Speech* (he uses his
voice). The fact that both demonstrations have exactly
the same purposes and results, and that speech is the
more exciting of the two, makes no difference. A
daughter wounds her father with a stiletto — *Action*.
The six-year-old girl in *A Celebrated Case,* by repeating her murdered mother's dying words: "Darling,
I am with your father," sends that innocent father to
the galleys — *Speech*. A hangman tightens a noose —
Action. The truth-telling nun's lying "Yes" in *The
Two Orphans* sends a doomed girl to liberty and an
uncondemned girl to the guillotine — *Speech*.

A playgoer may think that any movement of the
human body, or of any noticeable part of it, is an act.
My own definition of action in drama excludes many
such movements and includes many things which the
average playgoer would classify as speech. When I
want a term for action in the playgoer's sense, I shall
refer to it as nominal or so-called action. The first thing
to be said is that there is no logical distinction between
so-called action and speech. A man, rising from a chair,
lifts his body from the ground. Is that action? Certainly. Without rising, he lifts his arm or his leg. Action? Yes. He lifts his hand or his foot. Action? Yes.
He lifts his finger. Yes — after a second's thought. He
lifts his eyelid. Yes — reluctantly. His eyebrow? Yes —

rebelliously (after all, it's something, and it isn't speech). Very well. He lifts his upper jaw, he lifts his lip, and he pronounces a word. Action? The philosopher and the anatomist must answer "Yes."

Why is this "Yes" so difficult to say? Because we are not interested in these movements of the jaw and lip as movements; we are interested only in the sounds which they produce. Why in the sounds and not in the movements? Because the sounds tell us something of the speaker's mind. If the movements did as much, if the lip *curled* instead of framing a letter, that, too, would interest us. Indeed, it must be freely granted that, where a choice between means is possible, movement in nine cases out of ten expresses more than words. This is not because the imagination is more impressible by sights than sounds; were this true, music would be a less imaginative art than painting, and a visible word (i. e., a word in script or print) would be more impressive than its spoken counterpart. Both these notions are contrary to fact. The reason why we respond to expressive sights more willingly than to expressive sounds is that speech employs a system of arbitrary signs called an alphabet, whereas gesture (an insufficient word, but let it pass) uses natural signs, signs in which nature, not convention, furnishes at once both the impulse toward the act and the key to its interpretation. When the sound ceases to be conventional, the distinction vanishes. A laugh is just as theatrical as a gesture.

Textbooks are liberal of examples of the inferiority of words to movements in the matter of expressiveness. "I'll thrash you," says less than a shaken fist. "Come here" is less powerful than a beckon. "Take notice" is meaningless beside a wink. In the presence of a shrug, a yawn, vocabulary grovels. When we wish to express worthlessness, we snap our fingers — at the dictionary. The word "supercilious" as a substitute for the act makes us lift our eyebrows. The act of touching the finger to the forehead divests the *word* "insanity" of half its power. Compare "I kiss your hand" at the close of a Spanish letter with the act.

All this is convincing, and merits cordial emphasis; but we must not be wheedled into the belief that this superiority is absolute, that it is necessary, or even universal. Cases occur where speech outvalues movement. Finger on lip is stronger than "Hush" or "Be still"; it is less strong than the abnormally forcible "Shut up." "Halt" is a forceful word — more forceful probably than the correlated gestures. The lifting of priestly hands is more impressive than the text of most benedictions; but "The peace of God which passeth all understanding" affects me more than any gesture. We have no bodily movements which match the vigor of our imprecations. "Damn you" and "Go to hell" have no equivalents in the field of gesture. Nothing in the nature of words keeps them from rising to the impressiveness of movements.

In comparing speech with so-called action, we tend

to compare this action with its own reflection in speech, i. e., with narrative. But this comparison is most unfair, because narrative is one among many forms of stage speech, and is commonly a feeble form. We quote:

> Upon my secure hour thy uncle stole,
> With juice of cursed hebenon in a vial.

The difference between the word and the visible transaction is rightly felt to be immense, but from this sure ground we proceed to the thoughtless assumption that the same inferiority pertains to Hamlet's cry:

> By heaven! I'll make a ghost of him that lets me.

But this word of Hamlet's is not the spectrum or attenuation of a fact; it is a fact itself, a fact in its own right, a granule of history, and, what is more, a step in a progressive movement. Probably less than nineteen-twentieths of stage speech is subject to the devastating ordeal of comparison with an offstage act which it reports.

A speech may be many things; it may be an assertion, an expression of feeling, an incident, an occurrence, an event, a disaster, almost a catastrophe. I adduce examples.

Assertion:

> Now spurs the lated traveller apace
> To gain the timely inn.

Expression of feeling:

> Qu'il mourût. (From Corneille's *Horace*.)

Incident:

HEDDA. Look there! She has left her old bonnet lying about on a chair. (Miss Tesman, now in the room, owns the bonnet.)

Occurrence:

MENAS (*to Pompey*)
These three world-sharers, these competitors,
Are in thy vessel; let me cut the cable.
(The mere proposition is an occurrence.)

Event:

LEAR (*to Regan*)
To thee and thine, hereditary ever,
Remain this ample third of our fair kingdom.
(Not mere report, but actual bestowal.)

Disaster:

MAGDA (*to Schwartz*). How do you know that he was the only one? ("The terrible line which," Mr. Shaw says, "strikes the Colonel dead.")

Catastrophe:

BERNICK (*from behind the door, to Krap*). The "Indian Girl" is to sail. (An order and revocable; hence not, perhaps, a full catastrophe.)

The last five instances are acts, and they are words; the inference is unmistakable. This is no squeamish critic's finical distinction; it is backed by common usage. In real life a plea, a charge, a testimony, is an act; a verdict is an act; a sentence is an act: all are accomplished by words. An edict, a ukase, is an act; we talk fluently of acts of Congress, acts of Parliament. A proclamation made up of nothing more drastic than words may inspire a revolt and divide a kingdom. To propose, to accept, to decline, marriage is an act; to jilt is an act: the vehicle of all these acts is words. Are we told of the impressiveness of movement? Speech is movement. How does a man win a suit in law or love? By speech. How does he learn that that suit is won or lost? By speech again.

Speech, on or off the stage, may be action. What is dramatic action? A play is a series of states of mind, of changing states of mind; or rather, it is a means of acquainting us with such a series. Action occurs upon the stage when any pointed change in mental states is communicated to the audience by some clear and forcible means. It occurs whenever the dramatist brings home to us an angle, switch, or tack in the psychology. Actors have both bodies and voices, and, where a choice is possible, the body usually brings the mental shift more vividly before us than the voice. Hence the very proper emphasis on bodily movements, and the soundness of the growing interest in stage directions and in stage directorship. Trouble begins when we confound the preferred means with the end, when we insist that movement is identical with action.

I act when I say to you on stage or off: "Your father is a murderer," or "Your wife is a harlot." That is not conversation, not discourse; that is conduct. It is conduct (or action), because it works a mental revolution in the hearer.

This doctrine is open to a simple but convincing test. Granting its truth, all bodily movements on the stage that are not interpretative, that offer no clues to changing mental states, should be ineffectual and tiresome. Let us put a question or two. Why is no work ever done upon the stage even in working places at working hours by working people? Why is work left out even when its propriety is manifest, and its absence is a wrong to probability? Why would a stage director shudder at the thought of letting a wood sawyer saw wood for five successive minutes on the stage? Why is a stage typist never permitted to suspend her flirtations long enough to strike fifty consecutive keys? Because bodily movement without meaning, unrevealing, uncommunicative movement, is duller than the dullest harangue which a recriminating audience ever visited with groans and hisses. Movement is sometimes action. When? Speech is sometimes action. When? Is it not clear that the answer to both questions is the same, that either becomes action when it becomes the forceful indicator of a pointed mental change?

Two further re-enforcing points must not be slighted. There are cases where things even less palpable than speech may have all the virtue, all the potency, of action. At the close of the first act of Lonsdale's *Aren't We All?* the tempted husband gives the first kiss to the siren. The wife appears, sees the kiss, looks on in silence while the curtain falls. There are two bodily movements in this situation, but what affects us is our sight of the wife's sight of the transgression. Sight as an agent is far less palpable than speech; yet let it once become the clue to an upheaval in a woman's mind, and it puts on all the properties of action. Stranger yet, we may be powerfully affected without the aid of vision if we merely know that somebody behind the scenes is seeing something that recasts the shape of life. In Bulwer's *Richelieu* the young spendthrift and rioter De Mauprat is sent into a room offstage to face the executioner. What he really meets is his ladylove and destined wife, whom the wily and sportive old ecclesiastic has substituted for the grimmer apparition. We are moved as if by action, yet the cause is neither speech nor movement, but the *idea* of a *sight*.

Silence is at times almost a variety of speech. It is evidence of two of the most affecting conditions in the world, guilt and death; as such, the mental changes which it induces or evinces may be revolutionary. When this happens, it acts. In Schiller's *Maid of Orleans,* after the coronation at Rheims Joan's peasant father accuses her before the court of witchcraft. Successively her friends implore her for denial; successively she declines to speak; successively their terrors and misgivings grow. Silence is damning, and to damn is to act. Silence by its very nothingness is the culminating proof that anything that makes us realize a drastic mental change is action.

Let me guard very briefly against four misconceptions. First, I most emphatically do not want tame drama; I deplore the diminution of excitement on the contemporary stage. Secondly, I do not want more psychology. I think contemporary drama shoulders all the psychology that it can carry; *Strange Interlude* shoulders rather more. Thirdly, I do not think that means are indifferent. Means in drama are next to all-important. Pointed mental change is worthless without pointed indication of that change. Fourthly, I have no quarrel with the extensive use of so-called action — movements of bodies or of properties — on the contemporary stage. I do indeed think that its vogue has confused our thinking; and the object of this essay is not to alter practice, but to remedy confusion.

THE SOURCE OF PLEASURE IN
FAMILIAR PLAYS

⇝⇝⇝⇝⇝⇝⇝⇝⇝⇝⇝⇝⇝⇝⋙⋘⇜⇜⇜⇜⇜⇜⇜⇜

Why do we enjoy old plays? Why do we watch with pleasure the dramatic presentation of stories of which the issue and the chief events are foreseen from the outset?

Mr. William Archer, in his interesting book *Playmaking: A Manual of Craftsmanship,* draws a sharp distinction between curiosity, which pursues the unknown, and dramatic interest, which "survives when curiosity is dead." In support of this thesis, he alleges several indisputable facts. He says, in substance, that a familiar play is full of unfamiliar points, that structure — craftsmanship — is most appreciated in repetition, that known characters, even known jokes, have the privileges and welcome of old friends, that "our pleasure consists of a delicate blending of surprise with realized anticipation," that we are capable of a vicarious curiosity dependent on the fiction of ignorance. The acting is supposed to be merely competent, and the field is thus cleared for the analysis of other elements.

On these clearly sound if not clearly original points another man might have been content to rest his case, but Mr. Archer has an argument in reserve, an argument for which he claims much weight and a qualified originality. It is in thus leaving his intrenchments and taking the field that he exposes himself to attack, and it is no more than just to present his idea in his own lucid and supple English. He is speaking of the screen scene in *The School for Scandal*.

The greater part of our pleasure arises precisely from the fact that we know what Sir Peter and Charles do not know, or, in other words, that we have a clear vision of all the circumstances, relations, and implications of a certain conjuncture of affairs, in which two, at least, of the persons concerned are ignorantly and blindly moving toward issues of which they do not dream. We are, in fact, in the position of superior intelligences contemplating, with miraculous clairvoyance, the stumblings and fumblings of poor blind mortals straying through the labyrinth of life. Our seat in the theater is like a throne on the Epicurean Olympus, whence we can view with perfect intelligence, but without participation or responsibility, the intricate reactions of human destiny. (Page 171.)

An earlier utterance to the same purport is cited in a footnote (I quote in part only).

Curiosity is the accidental relish of a single night, whereas the essential and abiding pleasure of the theater lies in foreknowledge. In relation to the characters in the drama, the audience are as gods looking before and after. Sitting in the theater we taste, for a moment, the glory of omniscience. (Pages 171–172, note.)

"The glory of omniscience" is a vivid phrase, and it is well perhaps to remind ourselves that, in the present context, omniscience means nothing more than the knowledge, at second hand, of possibly a dozen, possibly three or four dozen, facts bearing on a single fictitious transaction.

The theory appeals, at first sight, to our experience of human nature. The appetite and the credulity of vanity are enormous and indiscriminate; we derive pleasure from the smallest of our real superiorities, and likewise from the least plausible of those imaginary superiorities in which so many of our real inferiorities are comprised. But even our grounds or excuses for self-complacence have their limits, and I do not think that we plume ourselves in relation to our fellow man except where we are entered in the same competitions, listed, in sporting parlance, for the same events. Thus I felicitate myself at the theater when I foresee an outcome or perceive a joke in advance of my fellow auditors; this is natural enough, for we are all ex officio competitors in the race for enlightenment. Again, I love to see my superiority attested by the follies and fatuities of the laughingstocks in comedy; I find in the drunkenness of Sir Toby Belch an embellishment of my own sobriety, in the ineptitudes of Sir Andrew Aguecheek an advertisement of my common sense. It is true that Sir Toby and Sir Andrew are, for anything I know, fictitious; but they purport to be copies of real originals, and Shakespeare, the actors, and myself are all in a conspiracy to pass them off as actualities. Viewed as such, they are in the same plane of opportunity with myself: they were free to follow their perverse instincts, or to take example by my temperance and wisdom.

The case is altered, however, when I pride myself on my superiority to Othello on the ground that I know his own story better than he does. How have I gained this superiority? I have seen the play, read the book, or been forewarned by some spectator or reader. Now in comparison with other persons who might have seen the play, read the book, or gossiped with their neighbors, and have proved derelict to all these opportunities (assuming knowledge of this kind to dignify its possessor), I am entitled no doubt to a genial self-complacency. But how is Othello himself to be brought within this category? The difficulty Othello must have had in reading or seeing or even discussing the play which bears his name is so manifest that, when I am asked to look down on him for his failure, even my vanity, which has never incurred the reproach of squeamishness, recoils from the crudity of the repast. In real life, indeed, a man who sees the whole of a situation of which others see only halves is justifiably elated; the others might have had the same wit or the same luck. But where knowledge is impossible, its absence ceases to be humiliating.

The principle may be stated thus: when a man compares himself with the effigies of men in imitative works of art, he gets no comfort out of superiorities arising solely out of his station as observer and their

position as objects of regard. In a gallery of im-
movable statues a man never meditates gloatingly on
his ownership of a pair of serviceable legs; before the
silence of Titian's doges or Raphael's saints he never
exults in the activity of his larynx. The same thing
applies to characters in history: a contemporary states-
man — Mr. Asquith, for example — reading the biography of Lord Grey or Mr. Gladstone would not
commend himself for superiorities of knowledge dependent solely on the elucidative influence of time;
he would exult where he felt that he could have made
better use of their data.

We not only revisit great plays with enthusiasm; we
re-read great novels with delight. The *rationale* of these
two facts must be almost identical, and Mr. Archer's
explanation, if valid, should be capable of transference
from the play to the novel. Now I must confess my
personal inability to carry over the idea of godship from
the theater to the book. I can, with some difficulty,
pursuant to Mr. Archer's flattering suggestion, imagine
myself a god in the theater; I can take my seat for a
throne in the same spirit in which Falstaff took his
"joined stool" for a "state" and his leaden dagger
for a golden scepter; and the presence of real people
in a removed precinct in a phase of life unrelated to
my own existence gives color to the sense of apotheosis.
But my throne is, both literally and metaphorically,
fastened to the floor of the theater; I cannot take it
home with me and survey the characters in *Jane Eyre*
or *Tess of the D'Urbervilles* or *The Rise of Silas*

Lapham from its dignified, if somewhat straitened, eminence. The visual and tangible supports for Mr. Archer's Olympian metaphor, the apparatus of godship, so to speak, are withdrawn; and I find myself unable to sustain the metaphor in the absence of these re-enforcements. When narrative is substituted for presentation, when the performance becomes entirely and manifestly subjective, I find myself incapable of rejoicing in the fact that I know more of a certain subject than certain other people who are obviously mere figments in my own mind. Yet the review of a great novel revives the original emotion quite as successfully as the return to a great play.

The instances of foreknowledge adduced by Mr. Archer are worth citing.

When Othello comes on the scene, radiant and confident in Desdemona's love, our knowledge of the fate awaiting him makes him a hundred times more interesting than could any mere curiosity as to what was about to happen. It is our prevision of Nora's exit at the end of the last act that lends its dramatic poignancy to the beginning of the first.

No apter illustrations of the sound doctrine that foresight may heighten interest could be adduced; but surely literature could be raked from one end to the other without finding an instance more adverse than that of Othello to the theory that the interest of foresight is based on the pride of knowledge. With slightly lessened emphasis the same thing might be reaffirmed of Nora Helmer. The interest is sympathetic, not personal; and the knowledge humbles rather than exalts. Does the group outside the window in Maeterlinck's *Intérieur* — no bad symbol, by the way, of the fore-warned audience in tragedy, in its sympathetic consciousness of the death of the girl of which no one as yet has ventured to apprise the peaceful family — does that group solace itself with the thought of its command of the situation?

Mr. Archer's Olympian theory is seen to be highly questionable, but the validity of his earlier arguments remains unaffected by the doubts that arise as to his supplementary hypothesis. Will not those earlier arguments suffice to explain the great and real pleasure we take in the revival of good plays? First of all, let us not exaggerate the stringencies of the problem. That a source of vivid and interesting emotion should be capable of eliciting vivid and interesting emotion on a second trial is no astonishing or anomalous fact; on the contrary, it is almost the rule. We do not drop a pear after the first mouthful, nor a jasmine after the first whiff; we swim or skate long after the novelty has vanished; we pace many times along a sea beach or through a portico; we visit more than once a cataract or a campanile; we find yearly pleasure in what Lowell called "the familiar novelty" of spring, "none the less novel, when it arrives, because it is familiar." Why should moving sections of human life be less qualified than other things to please and stir us in the absence of curiosity? In point of fact, in our living individual experience, the review of past excitements, where curiosity in its primitive form is impossible, ranks high among the recreations and solaces of life.

A knowledge of the outcome is less inhibitory than people fancy. The news of a disaster or stroke of good fortune often reaches us by the following gradations: a telegram, a letter, a personal colloquy. Does the telegram remove our wish to see the letter? Does the letter extinguish our desire for the interview? Why does a newspaper, so palpably and palpitantly anxious to cater to the suspense of its great infant, the public, never hesitate to let out its precious secret in the four or five words of an anticipatory headline? Simply because, in poignant affairs, a knowledge of essentials does not remove, but on the contrary stimulates, an interest in details.

Between these cases and that of the revisited play, a difference, in theory at least, must be admitted; in the play the spectator not only knows the issue but has already seen the particulars. But he has grasped them, or has grasped at them, hurriedly, casually, inadequately, under the strain of a violent and engrossing preoccupation with the outcome. Mr. Archer, in an altogether different context, speaks of the letter of which one takes in "the import, almost without reading the words." A moving drama might be compared to a momentous letter of which the first reading — the reading that tears the heart out of it — is careless because it is eager, and of which every syllable, almost every stroke, is sedulously conned on a second, more deliberate, perusal.

On the first night curiosity is paramount, to an extent which makes it hard to conceive that interest could survive the abstraction of this dominating factor. But the formula for the interest of the second night — assuming, for the sake of simplicity, that the visits are consecutive — is not simply: interest of the first night minus curiosity. It reads rather: interest of the first night minus curiosity plus interest (or, if you please, secondary curiosity) in a mass of detail passed by or half apprehended in the tension of the opening night. Let us figure to ourselves a group of associates dominated by a brilliant and copious talker; the observations of his companions in his presence might be merely casual and unimportant. But does it necessarily follow that, if the protagonist were called away, the ensuing conversation would sink to the incidental and trivial level of the previous forth-puttings of his interlocutors? Not in the least: the conversation of the leader had, probably enough, both stimulated and repressed the desire to speak in the minds of his associates; his withdrawal might be the signal for the emergence of new alacrities. In exactly the same way curiosity arouses secondary interests by the very conduct which precludes their immediate gratification; its recession is their opportunity. They are concerned in part with literary merits, more largely with craftsmanship, more largely still with emotional solicitations passed by or slurred over in the first eagerness of curiosity.

We pass to a group of facts illustrative of a further principle. A rustic surveys a country road with new eyes if he has once traced that road to its destination in the metropolis. A boatman watches the upper course of a stream with quickened interest if he has once followed its current to its far-off confluence with the ocean. A biologist studies the crude origins of life with heightened curiosity when he foresees their terminus in man. A boy reads with interest the commonplace opening chapters of a biography because he knows these things to have issued in achievement. An older man reads of the humble folkmoots in Friesland or Sleswick (the headwaters of the mighty river, as J. R. Green called them) or of those battles of kites and crows which Milton contemptuously pushed aside with a patience sustained by the distant but inspiring vision of a free commonwealth and a world-empire. These examples all point to the truth that a great known outcome irradiates all its antecedents, which, in turn, is part of the still wider principle that a great object glorifies its accessories. Admirable instances of the application of this truth to drama, particularly to tragedy, have been furnished by Mr. Archer himself in the references to *Othello* and *A Doll's House* quoted above; only Mr. Archer has attached to this undoubted truth a questionable theory of a satisfied thirst for omniscience on the part of a self-gratulating spectator. Our own list of examples of this anticipatory or retrospective interest—both adjectives, though formally contradictory, are in place—includes objects to which

Mr. Archer's theory is clearly inapplicable — objects like a road or a river with regard to which the idea of a competition in knowledge with a triumphant spectator is unthinkable. The principle, however, can dispense with the theory.

The universal hatred of monotony is curiously qualified with a fondness for an ascertained order. Children insist on verbatim repetitions of the nursery tale and resent the displacement of the humblest particular. The lover of good verse is scandalized by a misquotation. The slight variations in the Lord's Prayer shock ears to which they are unfamiliar. Every detail of a venerated ritual is anticipated and enjoyed by the pious. The recurrence in spring of the pasque flowers, the Dutchman's-breeches, and the bloodroot in the same spot and the same order is a pleasure which variation would disturb. The verification of forecast in the visit to the old home is a delight that cheapens novelty. The fact that variety is the only means by which the frequent repetition of unattractive processes can be made tolerable is thoroughly consistent with the principle that where objects are agreeable and repetitions rare perfect correspondence is the desideratum. Mr. Archer himself speaks aptly of the "delicate blending of surprise and realized anticipation" in the familiar play. The punctual arrival of each situation, each outcry, each jest, each metaphor, at the specified and anticipated time, the checking up of one's remembered goods and chattels, the sureness with which the immitigable Shakespeare or Ibsen or Bernard Shaw brings these willful actors and evasive managers to time, the delightful certainty with which these caprices and vagaries and insurgencies evolve to the foreseen and wished-for end — these things create a pleasure which unites in its fashion the charms of ordered plan and opportune coincidence.

The sum of the pleasures above cited might seem a sufficient compensation for the withdrawal of curiosity. But is it necessary to suppose that curiosity is inoperative even in a familiar play? An "acute critic" quoted by Mr. Archer thinks that curiosity of a sort may be aroused in the informed spectator through his self-identification with "the discovering persons on the stage." It seems clear that another sort of vicarious curiosity is aroused in the foreseeing spectator by his self-identification with the discovering persons in the audience. To many persons it would scarcely seem extravagant to go a step further and concede even his identification with his old self — the self that first saw or read the drama.

The contradiction between curiosity and foreknowledge as logical concepts does not apply with anything like the same force to curiosity and foreknowledge as psychological states. Logically, we cannot want to know what we do know, but the end of human nature would seem to be the discomfiture of logic. The mental tension we call curiosity is not necessarily or normally the sequel of a careful investigation and precise ascertainment of the state of our knowledge. It is an instinctive response to certain signs or symptoms of uncertainty or incompleteness in objects or actions. The justness or soundness of these intimations, the actuality, in other words, of the uncertainty or incompleteness they suggest, is a matter that we cannot always stop to determine before yielding our minds to the spell of curiosity. Now when, in real life, we see men wooing or quarreling or cheating or conspiring — the kind of actions which the stage habitually reflects — we assume that what is unsettled is uncertain. We do not stop to test this assumption. Its validity is so nearly universal that a test is superfluous. What, then, naturally occurs when the stage presents us with an action with all those marks of incompleteness which in real life justify the unhesitating assumption that the result is unknown and that curiosity is warranted? We accept the suggestion, and the tension appears in automatic response to the accustomed provocations.

But we do know the issue, avers the objector. True: but this knowledge of the outcome, though, in one sense, a permanent possession of the mind, is by no means a permanent occupant of consciousness. Its emergences are normally few, and between its emergences it is inoperative. The thought of the end will come to us in a familiar play, but its staying with us is another matter. A mind preoccupied with an engrossing spectacle cannot be expected to occupy itself in rectifying the impressions of that spectacle by perpetual recourse to a counteractive, disillusioning, and, therefore, for the time being, unpalatable fact lurking somewhere in the outskirts of consciousness. My memory knows that Mercutio is slain by Tybalt. But how is my memory to get credence or even audience for its impertinent allegations when my eyes and ears are dominated by a brisk interchange of thrust and counterstroke upon the stage, absorbing in its interest and obviously undecided? When I have found out whether he is slain by Tybalt, I shall have leisure to remember that I knew it beforehand.

In the theater, where so much illusion is current, why should we chaffer over the illusion of uncertainty? If we can assume toward unreal things the attitude appropriate to reality, why cannot we assume toward known things the attitude appropriate to ignorance?

We see, then, that in a broad survey of life what has once affected us strongly usually has the power to affect us strongly again; we see that the satisfaction of the leading or initial curiosity is the needed occasion and signal for the emergence of strong secondary interests; that in many phases of life and literature alike the knowledge of a great outcome is an incalculable reenforcement of our interest in preliminaries: that a definite order becomes itself the object of a strong, even an exigent and jealous, affection; that, if we use our prerogative as human beings to throw over logic and resort to psychology, curiosity is found to coexist with knowledge. In the light of these considerations, all of which are briefly stated or indicated by Mr. Archer himself, it hardly seems necessary to climb Olympus with that distinguished critic — alluring as such a journey would undoubtedly be with such companionship — to obtain a point of view from which the interest in known plays becomes intelligible.

THE CHARACTER OF MACBETH

M R. BARRETT WENDELL in his book on Shakespeare emphasizes the interesting suggestion that there are gaps or omissions in our present version of *Macbeth* corresponding to the lost or unwritten parts of a larger and more varied play than that embodied in the current text. There may or may not be lacunae in the play: what is more certain and not less interesting is the presence of lacunae in the delineation of Macbeth. We feel that that delineation, vivid as it is, leaves many questions unanswered; whole tracts, great provinces, of his life and activity remain untouched in the representation. He is shown to us in a series of situations that are at once very extraordinary and somewhat monotonous. Action in the form of crime and retribution in the form of self-torture make up the bulk, almost the total, of his recorded experience. To see Kean was to read Shakespeare by flashes of lightning; it might be said that to read *Macbeth* is to observe the hero by lightning flashes. Kean's auditors may sometimes have wished for a ray or two of commonplace daylight; and the students of Macbeth's character would have liked to see him from time to time as he ate and drank, talked and trafficked, counseled and wrought, in the daily round of life.

I am far from asserting that the character is incoherent or incongruous; nothing more can be said than that Shakespeare is uncommunicative with respect to sundry parts of Macbeth's nature; a point is reached in the delineation where "the rest is silence." This no more implies a rupture or disjunction in the fabric of the man himself than the obscuration by fog of certain sections of a mountain slope implies a break in the cohesion of the ridge. Whether the hiatus in our conception represents a hiatus in Shakespeare's is a point not easy to determine. With us, as with Macbeth in the first encounter with the witches, revelation ends before curiosity is satisfied; the same cry which Macbeth utters to the Weird Women —

Stay, you imperfect speakers, tell me more—

we could almost repeat to Shakespeare. But are we sure that the witches knew more than they disclosed? And we are quite certain that Shakespeare knew much more of Macbeth than he has chosen to reveal to us. Would it not have been highly characteristic, highly Shakespearean, for the great dramatist, after choosing the events and situations to be portrayed, to vivify or vitalize in his inner vision the moral traits bearing on those events and situations, and to leave the rest in total obscurity or doubtful twilight? Was he not just the type of man to use the torch he carried no further than it threw light upon its path?

The study of Macbeth's character is hampered in another way by the comparative meagerness of his self-expression. Many readers would doubtless be surprised to learn how little Macbeth actually says. In the long and important third scene of the first act he speaks only thirteen times; in his first talk with his wife he speaks three times and utters fifteen words; in the hesitation scene that closes the first act he speaks seven times, once at great length; in the dagger scene he speaks six times; in the courtyard after the murder, a scene which expands in our excited minds to epical or cosmical dimensions, he speaks thirteen times; in the entire fifth act there are only twenty-six speeches.

It is obvious that a delineation on this scale, however ample for the imagination, is inadequate for purposes of analysis. It follows that the analytic faculty is obliged to husband its resources, to search out and utilize every shred and scrap of available material. Shakespearean scholarship, to make any progress at all with these meager materials, must proceed on the hypothesis that everything is a datum, that every word or movement, however minute, is a part of the testimony. In physical science such an hypothesis would be perfectly sound; there is no ascertainable fact about a stone or animal which may not, and should not, form a part of a perfect conception of that stone or animal. But in the study of Shakespeare a liberal mind becomes more and more convinced of the unsoundness of the presumption which attributes to every utterance of every character the maximum of intention and significance, while at the same time it perceives that under any other suppo-

sition progress in the unraveling of the more difficult
characters is impossible. In Shakespeare men speak
for many other ends than that of self-revelation;
there are plots to carry forward, poetry to declaim,
aphorisms to enunciate; they must enlighten audiences,
amuse groundlings, and compliment kings. Even this
leaves out of account the wide scope for accident and
negligence in a mind prone, as we can hardly doubt,
to take a liberal and lenient view of its own obligations
and shortcomings. One can readily fancy Shakespeare
as acting on the principle, which is in many ways a
sound and sagacious principle, that all kinds of men
do all sorts of things, and, where a given thing was
to be done or said, assigning it without too much
scruple to the actor occupying for the moment the
center of the stage.

The character of Macbeth furnishes a good illustration of the difficulty in question. The evidence for
many traits in the nature of Macbeth is confined to
single passages, occasionally to brief suggestions. The
imputation of avarice to the usurper in his decadence
rests upon one word in one speech in the mouth of an
enemy (Malcolm, in the third scene of the fourth act).
The imputation of profligacy rests upon exactly the
same basis. A single inconclusive speech in the fifth act
is our warrant for concluding that his affection for his
wife has materially declined. A single exclamation of
four words, "I would thou couldst!" is the sum of the
evidence we possess that he repented even momentarily

of any one of his murders. One speech and one only, "I dare do all that may become a man," breathes a clear note of manly rectitude. A sympathetic and reverential attitude toward virtue is displayed just once in the reference to the meek and angel-like virtues of the unhappy Duncan. In a single scene, the third of the fifth act, he rails and curses in a fashion to which there is no parallel and no near approach in the remainder of the play. The evidence of concern for his own soul is clear-cut but very meager. The evidence of tact and efficiency in the conduct of affairs which may be cited from the first part of the third act is small in amount and dubious in character. How much weight should be given to such meager and casual indications? It is hard to say. It seems unlikely that Shakespeare could mean that any trait should stand out strongly in our conceptions, or rather in the conceptions of his audience, unless it figured largely in the delineation. He did not draw men in cipher or cryptogram; he drew them largely, plainly, boldly, for the common untrained eye. On the other hand, if we assume that nothing is authentic which is not prominent, that nothing is discoverable which is not obvious, advance is barred and scholarship in this field becomes abortive.

My own view of the character of Macbeth is not revolutionary. I subscribe to most of the current opinions, and shall rather aim to insert my judgments in the clefts or interstices of the accepted notions than to overturn or displace them. I am prepared to admit that Macbeth's physical courage was unquestionable, that he was ambitious and unprincipled, that he probably entertained the thought of murder before the meeting with the witches, that his character rapidly degenerates in the last acts, that his love for his wife, at first of singular tenderness and intensity, is later somewhat impaired, that his chief point of distinction from the vulgar usurper and assassin is a vivid, poetical, masterful imagination.

The last point, however, deserves a somewhat fuller investigation. In respect to the gloomy and restricted nature of the imagination of Macbeth I should say that I was in entire accord with the ablest of recent scholars, if agreement itself were not a species of presumption in relation to a critic of the stamp of Dr. Bradley. Two points, however, have scarcely received the attention which they merit — the cosmic or boundless quality of this imagination, and its unrivaled fixity and tenacity. Macbeth sees things in their breadth or infinity. His thoughts are "broad and general as the casing air," and to be cribbed or confined is the type of unbearable torture. The whole "half-world" with its aggregated misdeeds rises before his vision as he waits in the court-yard for the bell that summons him to the murder. The whole sea is present to his imagination when he looks despairingly at the hands that all Neptune's ocean cannot wash clean. His fancy sees the lines of Banquo's descendants stretching out to the "crack of doom," and the succession of blank tomorrows reaching to "the last syllable of recorded time." He views the commotions of the elements less from the station of the petty mundane beholder than from the point of vantage of a superhuman observer commanding the entire breadth of the planet.

But the concentration of this picture-making power is hardly less remarkable than its sweep. If I had to express the truth in metaphor, I should say that his imagination had talons. There is a grip, a clutch, an insistence, a tenacity, in his mental processes, which suggests the idea of possession. An image conquers, masters, enslaves, engrosses him; he is in its leash; he obeys and cringes. Sight has for him the power of touch: the crown sears his eyeballs; the bloody hands pluck out his eyes. He cannot rid himself of a visual image; the imaginary dagger side by side with the real one which he has drawn to disprove its existence retains its actuality. If the murderer had merely told him that Banquo was dead, Macbeth would have seen no ghost at the supper. It was the addition of the picturesque adjuncts:

> Safe in a ditch he bides,
> With twenty trenched gashes on his head

that wrought the mischief. The murderer spoke of twenty gashes: Macbeth speaks of "twenty mortal murders on their crown": a clear proof that the phantom is only the materialization of the terrible image which the murderer's words had etched upon that receptive and tenacious brain. The importunity, the inveteracy, of certain sense impressions is one of the memorable points in his constitution. The first prophecy of the witches, the imaginary voice calling "Sleep no more," the thought of Birnam wood and the immunity from all born of women, infix and imbed themselves in the tissues of his fantasy to an extent which makes him forgetful of his surroundings and insensible to the gravest perils.

His imagination is penal and retributive, as every reader at once perceives; but it is not a source of un-mixed pain. There is an awe not unmixed with charm in the solemn and mysterious relation which the crimes of Macbeth establish between his own soul and the great material and moral forces in the cosmos, earth, the stars, night, heaven, and hell; and Macbeth was the man of all others to feel and value that awe. It is hard to believe that he could have pronounced the famous passage describing the descent of night, "ere the bat hath flown his cloister'd flight," etc., perhaps the finest lines of their kind in literature, without sharing in the profound and melancholy pleasure with which Shakes-peare wrote, and every reader reads, these lines. There is a passage in the dagger scene which brings out this trait with extraordinary clearness. Macbeth entreats the earth to muffle his steps. Now there is a very obvious and weighty reason why an assassin should value silence, and we are so much under the yoke of this idea that we can read the passage more than once without noticing that Macbeth has given his own rea-

son for his wish and that that reason is entirely different from the one in our minds. Macbeth fears that the
sounds

> will take the present horror from the time
> Which now suits with it.

In other words, he feels an artistic and dramatic propriety in the silence, the removal of which would inter-
fere with the esthetic enjoyment of the situation. The
retention of any care for poetical and artistic fitness in
that crucial and appalling moment is the mark of what
we might almost call the epicure in crime. It might
have furnished De Quincey with a point for his "Murder as One of the Fine Arts." That this pleasure is in
any degree commensurate or even comparable with the
suffering which it accompanies, no man in his senses
would assert; but its mere existence is noteworthy and
enlightening.

Another trait which it is impossible to overlook and
yet easy to undervalue is Macbeth's inclination to
brooding, abstraction, profound reverie, bordering
upon trance. In the first scene with the witches, the
word "rapt" is twice applied to Macbeth, the first
occasion arising only eight lines below the point at
which the third witch has uttered the momentous and
fatal ascription. In the latter part of the scene he remains so long engrossed in thought that even his
respectful companions are obliged to waive their deference far enough to remind him of the need of expe-
dition. In the dagger scene he is again submerged in

his own reflections; in the courtyard scene with Lady Macbeth, where the motives to action and speed are peremptory, his words carry with them a sense of distance and solitude as if they rose from the depths of a well or the gratings of a stronghold. More remarkable still, perhaps, is the drop from the fiery vehemence of his challenge and defiance to the spirit of Banquo to the mood of tranquil and dreamlike reverie suggested in the words:

> Can such things be,
> And overcome us like a summer's cloud,
> Without our special wonder?

lines almost mimetic of the "tranced summer calm" of the still white cloud in the peaceful heavens. The third scene of the fifth act is highly suggestive in its picture of the sudden transition from moods of frantic violence to the calmness of deep and melancholy abstraction. We are somewhat blinded to the frequency and significance of episodes like these by the fact that Macbeth is a warrior and a sovereign, and that his reveries are interspaced by sudden, drastic, and decisive actions.

We might expect that Macbeth's reflections would be confined to the state of his own mind and fortunes. We are surprised, however, to find in this brawny Scotch thane with his soldierly prowess and his political ambition a tendency to generalize, to reason from himself to mankind, and from his own experience to life in the aggregate. Macbeth is fond of the impersonal "we," the "we" that stands for the race, or a large section of humanity. "We still have judgment here," "we but teach bloody instructions," "can such things be, and overcome us," "all our yesterdays have lighted fools." He coins aphorisms: "present fears are less than horrible imaginings," "the labour we delight in physics pain," "bloody instructions . . . return to plague the inventor," "vaulting ambition . . . o'erleaps itself," "the flighty purpose never is o'ertook unless the deed go with it," "life's but a walking shadow," "who dares do more is none." He can generalize about sleep in a moment of anguish; Banquo's ghost has been gone but half a second before he has so far mastered his frenzy as to be able to draw a distinction between present and past times in the matter of the reappearance of dead bodies. Even in the last act, when his egotism is untrammeled, when his self-engrossment has reached a point where it begins to encroach on the one great unselfish passion of his soul, his love for his wife, he is still capable of throwing his thoughts into form which makes their compass as wide as the race. It is the life of all men which he likens to the poor player and the idiot's tale.

Another feature of these reflective passages is the ingenuity and dexterity of the expression, the trimness and expertness of both the logical and the literary form. Macbeth's thoughts on the witches' salutation embody themselves in the following shapely and pointed dilemma and antithesis:

> This supernatural soliciting
> Cannot be ill; cannot be good: if ill,
> Why hath it given me earnest of success,
> Commencing in a truth? I am thane of Cawdor:
> If good . . .

A French stylist could not have turned the phrases more deftly. And this is done under what circumstances? When, as Macbeth tells us, with a calm method in itself suggestive, his hair is standing on end and his seated heart is knocking at his ribs. To all of which he has equanimity enough to add the remark that these proceedings are against the uses of nature.

Observe, again, the perfect order, the luminous distinctions, in the strenuous soliloquy that opens the seventh scene of the first act. He makes a supposition contrary to fact, that murder has no earthly penalties, discusses and rejects it, then reverts to the opposite and authentic supposition. He goes on to state the case against the murder with a deftness and precision worthy of David Hume or Adam Smith:

> He's here in double trust:
> First, as I am his kinsman and his subject,
> Strong both against the deed; then, as his host,
> Who should against his murderer shut the door

In the first scene of the third act the separation of Banquo's qualities into two groups or planes and the superposition of one of these groups or planes upon the other (lines 49–54) are accomplished with equal dexterity. Another instance of this mastery of form is the unbending terseness of the famous

THE CHARACTER OF MACBETH

> I dare do all that may become a man;
> Who dares do more is none.

It is hardly safe to lay much stress on the cases of hyperbole and of aggregated and, as it were, aggravated metaphor, although their employment at a moment when Macbeth's earnestness is terrible, to wit, in the picture of the blessings of sleep, is sufficiently noteworthy. But this kind of rhetoric was so highly prized by Shakespeare for its own sake that its appearance in the mouth of any speaker hardly establishes its claim to a place in the roll of that speaker's characteristics. If the first speeches of Macduff after the discovery of the murder of Duncan had been assigned to Macbeth, I should certainly have held them up as a signal and admirable example of the fustian originating in hypocrisy, just as if Macbeth's lying speech, "the labour we delight in physics pain," had been put into the mouth of Banquo, I should have regarded it as a clear case of the directness and conciseness which sincerity imparts to candid utterance. Nevertheless, it is impossible to look upon the turgid rhetoric into which Macbeth is impelled by the stringencies of deceit as wholly devoid of significance. A man to whom such rhetoric was uncongenial would have contrived another screen: our choice of disguises is controlled by our real nature.

An interesting question meets us at this point. The three traits last noted, the brooding, the generalizing, the literary and logical form, carry with them a certain presumption of want of executive force, of relative inefficiency in action. On the other hand, Macbeth's success in arms, his kingship, and his prompt attainment of his leading object induce the opposite presumption. Which of these inferences is correct? Is Macbeth a real man of affairs, or is he a thinker and dreamer drifted out of his proper element?

The only traces I can find of intelligent and efficient action on the part of Macbeth occur in the first part of the third act, and are slight or equivocal. He may be dexterous, as Professor Bradley says, in extracting from Banquo the needful information with respect to his ride and his company; but surely one may overrate the amount of tact required for asking questions on the part of one who unites the claims of an old friend with a position which makes every inquiry a favor. He appears also to have carefully designed the murder of Banquo; but half his design, the removal of Fleance, entirely miscarries. Everywhere else he either hesitates or blunders. He lacks the moral and facial self-control indispensable to a strategist. His wife's ceaseless vigilance is required to prevent his absence of mind or absence of body on occasions where his presence in both modes is imperative. The company of his leading nobles at a state banquet is no check on an outburst of frenzy.

Again, Macbeth almost never shows the instincts or capacities of leadership. He is pushed into the murder of Duncan by a combination of fate, chance, and woman. After the discovery of the crime, the amazement and helplessness of the spectators and the demand for instant action should have served as a summons to whatever powers of initiative and kingship lay dormant in his untested nature. Macbeth cannot respond to the summons. It is true that after a time he offers the suggestion that the lords shall arm themselves and meet in the hall; but this is only in reply to a suggestion of Banquo, to whom he has passively abandoned the advantage of the initial step. This can hardly be attributed to consternation; for he has just braced himself to the incredible hardihood of guiding Macduff to Duncan's chamber, and of waiting at the threshold, chatting with Lenox about the night, until Macduff shall reappear with his fearful tidings. His wife faints, and he leaves the care of her to Macduff and Banquo.

The objects of his attack are chosen with singular ineptness. He permits the escape of Malcolm, who is a real and serious menace to his safety, while he marshals all his power and cunning against Banquo, who is apparently tolerant of the status quo. He allows Macduff to find an asylum in England and then indemnifies himself by the insensate and motiveless slaughter of his family. In the critical juncture in the fifth act he is without policy and without resource, except that of hugging to his soul the flattering unction of his delusive and beguiling oracles. In details he is equally impolitic. The choice of his own castle as the place for the slaughter of one antagonist is rivaled by the choice of his own park as the spot for the assassination of another. He appoints two men to commit a crime, and is then childish enough to add a third at the last moment without forewarning the original agents.

I am well aware that in matters of this kind it is possible to reason too hastily from the facts to intentions. Shakespeare's plotters are among his masterly portraits, yet the plotting itself is seldom masterly, and the acts of his villains sometimes fall far short of the craft and address implicit in their speech and bearing. The poet's standards of strategy were not high, and acts that are clearly impolitic may sometimes be assigned to perpetrators who were meant to be sagacious. Still, after all deductions, it is hard to picture Macbeth as the typical or even the competent man of action. It is true that he is neither idle nor irresolute. He does much, or at all events he is very busy; and, except in the case of Duncan, he decides promptly, and adheres to his decision. But in the true tests of executive force, the wise choice of ends and means, Macbeth is altogether deficient. The choice of wise ends is so far from being numbered among his faculties that he may scarcely be said in any proper sense to choose his ends at all. He is a man who waits for guidance, one of that large class who, in the words of another Shakespearean conspirator and assassin, take suggestion as a cat laps milk. The whole plot turns upon his wife's urgency. Throughout the first three acts he is engaged in carrying out the hints of the witches, and when by the accomplishment of the death of Banquo the stock of intimations is virtually exhausted, he resorts forthwith to the Weird Women for a new installment of suggestions.

Nor does his action appear to better advantage if tested by the choice of means. His efforts are wanting in that adjustment of deeds to perceptions which discriminates conduct from mere action. His deeds are the lurches and plunges of the distempered spirit, not the gallop but the rearing of the horse, under the spur; they are reliefs and distractions, anesthetics if you please, the endeavor of the racked nerves to find in action a sedative for thought. He resorts to murder as other men to opium; remorse or fear is slaked for the time being by the very drug which eventually renews it; and the second debauch is sought as an escape from the penalties of the first. These are truths old enough and clear enough to form part, as it were, of the patrimony of criticism.

What, then, was the nature of Macbeth's aspiration toward kingship? Was it a form of that powerful and often beneficial instinct which urges the man who can handle an oar or a rifle or a chisel to seek out a position that affords him the command of these implements? Richard III and Edmund are sovereigns by nature, and their conduct, diabolical as it is, may be viewed in one way as nature's effort to adjust situation to character. But it is the ownership rather than the exercise of power that captivates the fancy of Macbeth; if indeed we ought not to go still further and affirm that for him the regalia are the kingship. His ambition is not the strong man's craving for more scope and better tools, but the child's wish for the moon, the vague longing for the remote splendor.

The very small extent to which this ambition is really pictured in the play is a remarkable rather than a significant circumstance. The drama cannot be called a portrayal of the struggle between ambition and conscience or ambition and fear, for the simple reason that the ambition, though present and operative, is not portrayed. It is assumed, presupposed if you will; but depicted it is not. The representation of Macbeth's desire for kingship in his own words is confined to three sentences, all in the first act: the "happy prologue to the swelling act of the imperial theme," the brief but mighty phrase, "the greatest is behind," and one sentence in the letter to Lady Macbeth on the "dues of rejoicing" and the promised greatness. That is the compass of Macbeth's own portrayal of his ambition. It is noteworthy that most of the ringing and glowing phrases in reference to kingship in the latter half of the first act are assigned to Lady Macbeth. It is she who speaks of "the golden round," who terms kingship "the ornament of life"; and it is she who enunciates that massive and herculean phrase, the "solely sovereign sway and masterdom." It is worth noting, also, that her arguments in the hesitation scene are appeals not to ambition but to pride — the pride of the resolute and fearless man.

As a result of these facts, the portrayal of the incentives to the crime is so slight and incidental and the portrayal of the deterrents is so appallingly vigorous and vivid that the reader scarcely sees how the thing ever got itself done. In addition to this, not one moment of exultation in the successful completion of the deed, not one throb of satisfaction in the possession of the dearly bought kingship, is vouchsafed to either of the conspirators. Had a monk written this play instead of Shakespeare, it could not have been more austere or inflexible in its denial of happiness to the wicked.

The foregoing remarks are not meant to disprove the reality or the strength of Macbeth's ambition, but merely to point out its subordination in the scale of literary emphasis.

There are certain analogies between the characters of Macbeth and Hamlet which are not uninstructive for those who keep clearly in mind the limits of their scope and importance. They are akin in the tendency to brooding and abstraction, in the generalizing impulse, in the feeling for rhetorical and literary form, in the dependence on suggestion, in the absence of true executive faculty, in the reckless suddenness and precipitation of certain actions. The proportions of thought and action in the two natures are, indeed, reversed; thought with Macbeth is as occasional and transient as action with Hamlet. For Hamlet, thought is the staple of existence, and action is rarer and more difficult than with Macbeth, though, when once aroused, it is hardly less headlong and instinctive. Under ordinary circumstances they would not have understood each other; Macbeth would have called Hamlet a driveler, and Hamlet would have dubbed Macbeth a savage. But one can conceive of their meeting in special moods upon rare occasions when their hearts might have flowed together in the coalescence of an absolute sympathy.

A trifling incident from my own experience may serve to illustrate the affinity of certain moods and tones of the two characters. While this essay was in my mind, I chanced to find myself one evening at a performance of an inferior play by a stock company. Some obscure train of association or mere wandering of mind diverted my thoughts to the closing scenes of *Macbeth*. Amid the distractions of the representation, I tried to recall the words of the "tomorrow and to-morrow" passage, and found myself gliding insensibly from the "life's but a walking shadow" of *Macbeth* to the "'t is an unweeded garden" of the first soliloquy in *Hamlet*. Macbeth ends on the note of cynicism and disillusion on which Hamlet commences. Usually, though perhaps not in the above instance, Hamlet's thought is saner and more moral than Macbeth's. The latter sees the world, as it were, by the light of conflagration in the somber radiance of the flame kindled by his own destructive energies: Hamlet sees it in what is essentially common daylight, though clouded more or less by the vapors arising from his own restless and perplexed spirit.

The moral character of Macbeth is, in most points, tolerably clear. He is a very bad man, but is not quite so bad as his acts. His first crime is committed under external pressure: all the others under the goad of self-torture: hardly one is the deliberate outcome of his unclouded will and judgment. He is the weak man made bad through weakness; and the agony which a worse man would not have felt drives him forward into excesses which a worse man might have avoided. It follows that he is both more criminal and less depraved than the ordinary unthinking and unfeeling villain. The actual manifestations of goodness are decidedly fewer than the author might have introduced, had he so pleased, without loss to the interest or reality of the character. Except in relation to his wife, I cannot remember that Macbeth utters one word of absolutely unequivocal kindness to any human being.

This deficiency is the more remarkable, as by a curious inversion of what might have seemed historically probable and dramatically appropriate, Shakespeare has made the moral standards of the Scottish court surprisingly high. With the exception of Macbeth and his wife, the witches and the murderers, nearly every person in the play is marked by generosity and honor. The very lay figures are unmistakable gentlemen; and episodes like the gallantry of young Siward and the magnanimity of his father are flung into the play with an unconcern which suggests a time when heroism was too common to be memorable. All this is in impressive contrast with the brutal and barbaric environment of *King Lear* and the thinly veiled baseness and hypocrisy which is the moral atmosphere of the court in *Hamlet*.

The nature of Macbeth's scruples and the cause of his self-torture are capable of more than one interpretation. At the first glance, conscience seems to be but slightly concerned with either: the scruples appear to spring from expediency and the self-torture from fear. But Professor Bradley's idea that his conscience, inarticulate in its proper form, finds a voice or spokesman in his imagination, has a nobility and subtlety which dispose one to instant assent. There is beauty as well as inspiration in the thought that the moral sense, like Kent in *King Lear*, returns in a new form to watch over the interests of the soul from which in its proper shape it has been summarily ejected. If one hesitates a little, nevertheless, the misgiving appears less as a bar to assent than as a hindrance to comprehension. Conscience itself, especially in crude minds, is the disguise for so many motives that we are a little perplexed when we are asked to conceive of another sensation as the disguise of conscience. And is not imaginative horror, usually and normally, a composite sensation of which conscience is an ingredient? Does it not consist of a psychical recoil to which many elements, the fear of hell, the fear of law, the fear of shame, and sympathy for the victim, contribute in various degrees, typifying and embodying itself in the fearful external signs and tokens of sanguinary crime — the darkness, the silence, the blood, the death struggle, the pallor and fixity of the dead body? To my mind the ideas of conscience and imaginative horror are both complex, and cover in part the same ground; and a difficulty rather conceptual than logical presents itself in the attempt to picture one as the substitute or spokesman for the other.

A view of this kind enables us to lighten a very little our condemnation of Macbeth, and it is significant that the reader welcomes the possibility. There are things, however, that are harder to forgive than wickedness, and I am afraid that Macbeth cannot be acquitted of these more odious, if less heinous, attributes. Our efforts to respect him are continually foiled by the outcrop of a vein of meanness and littleness bordering upon sheer vulgarity. If he ever was a gentleman, that part of him died on the night when he murdered Duncan. After that event the depravation of his character is hardly more rapid or more manifest than the cheapening and coarsening which accompanies the moral decline. In his speech with the nobles in his court, there is to my ear a distinct note of what in vulgar American parlance is called "palaver," or, in an American parlance still more vulgar, "dope." He was far more kingly before he attained the crown. In his dialogue with the two murderers, there is a mixture of familiarity and vehemence, of bonhomie and solicitude, suggestive both

of an unkingly eagerness and of the ready fraterniza-
tion of the crowned cutthroat with his humbler brethren of the guild. When the witches at his own request
show him pictures which excite his alarm, he reviles
them in the dialect of a crossing-sweeper. An attend-
ant brings him bad news and he lashes him with scur-
rilities and maledictions. It is a far cry from the
chieftain who said to Ross and Angus

> Kind gentlemen, your pains
> Are register'd where every day I turn
> The leaf to read them

to the ruffian who bawls to his unoffending servant:

> The devil damn thee black, thou cream-faced loon!

And though in this case we must allow for variation
of mood as well as for degeneration of character, no
allowance can rob the change of its impressiveness.

There are other things of perhaps an even more
trenchant significance. Treachery is a normal adjunct
of murder, and it would be as vain to expect truth as
humanity from "the smyler with the knyf under the
cloke." But Macbeth is perfectly at home among all
the ignominies which his situation suggests or enforces.
He can stoop to the incredible meanness of reproaching
Banquo with unkindness for an absence the true cause
of which is at that very moment disturbing his guilty
heart. A still more aggravated case is his stirring appeal
to Lady Macbeth:

> Bring forth men-children only;
> For thy undaunted mettle should compose
> Nothing but males.

The reader who forgets the context naturally supposes that this is the reply to some peculiarly daring and heroic utterance on the part of the lady. It is with a shock that, on turning to the book, he discovers the actual nature of the proposition to which this outburst of enthusiasm is the reply. That proposition is the revolting and despicable suggestion that the faces of the grooms in the sleeping-chamber shall be smeared with blood and the crime laid at the door of these luckless menials. This is what strikes Macbeth as " undaunted mettle." There is a baseness in these things that transcends the baseness inherent in the very nature of assassination. We cannot discern in the guilty Macbeth the features of that darkened and ruined archangel whom Milton likened to the thunderstricken oak on the "blasted heath"; he appears to us rather in the likeness of the later embodiments of that versatile spirit, creeping like the serpent or squat like the toad.

Macbeth shows a selfish and common nature driven by circumstances and urgency to the perpetration of a deed which he was neither strong enough nor bad enough to have committed without prompting, and the weight of which, once committed, he is not strong enough or bad enough to sustain. He becomes, in Middleton's vivid characterization of another murderer, " the deed's creature "; he cannot escape from its yoke or its shadow. He is worse than wicked; he is small: yet at his worst and smallest he is capable of regaining for the moment our sympathy, almost our respect, by the awe-struck earnestness, the solemnity, of the regard which he turns upon himself and destiny. At the crisis of his fate, when the crown and the head under it are both at stake, he arraigns life on the ground, not that it is cruel or terrible, but that it is petty and meaningless. Could crime have made life stale or tedious to any mind not by nature predisposed to find its substance and its interest in virtue? We divine the latency of high possibilities; we feel that his spiritual ear is laid close to the inmost shrine of far deeper oracles than those which have tantalized and beguiled him; we suspect that a nature that could make its way through crime to wisdom or at least to thought might, under happier auspices, have retraced the path from contemplation back to virtue. The light, it is true, is dim and transitory, less valuable in itself than for the glimpse it affords of a profound seriousness, which asserts, even from the crime and meanness of the im-bruted spirit in which it has made its transient house, its inalienable fellowship with virtue and greatness.

WHAT HAPPENED TO HAMLET?
A NEW PHASE OF AN OLD VIEW

THE theory of Hamlet which the present essay sub-
mits is nothing very new — is, in fact, nothing but a
new posture of the classic Coleridgian judgment that
Hamlet signifies the inhibition of executive force by
intellectual activity. In a question in which debate is
old, theories are fragile in the ratio of their novelty.
The inadequacy of the old theories, which is implied
in the permanence of the problem, drives men to seek
relief and respite in the greater and more glaring inadequacy of the new. But disproof or distrust quickly
overtakes them, and they return from the new to the
old, from the greater dissatisfaction to the less, as Lear,
who wanted a hundred knights, returned to Goneril:

> Thy fifty yet doth double five-and-twenty,
> And thou art twice her love.

The truth is that no single theory can disentangle
Hamlet. The difficulties in the case are quite peculiar.
Hamlet is insane or feigns insanity through most of
the play, and it is clear that insanity or its counterfeit
will rob speeches of all or most of their cogency as signs
of character. If the remaining material — the material
we can absolutely trust — is at the same time stinted
and diversified, the problem is scarcely soluble. More-

over, the Shakespearean conception of Hamlet appears to have been, in a quite exceptional degree, *unfenced*. The barrier which kept the characteristic from straying out and the uncharacteristic from slipping in was unusually weak. In a sense, this means an approximation to nature, because character, as we know it in literature, is always a convenient simplification of the facts. A character is a man made intelligible by abridgments and emendations. In Hamlet the abridging and emending process has been scanted, and the character reverts to its inherent diversity and obscurity.

The worst of theories, however, has a value, because it presents the old facts in a new grouping. And an old fact in a new relation is half new. The old theory is safe; the new is savory: and a combination of the new and the old way may, in a fashion, combine savor with safety. I proceed, therefore, without further delay, to my variation of Coleridge, which is reducible to a single sentence: Hamlet did not *lose* his mind, but *found* it, in the shock of catastrophic revelation, and in the excitement — almost the exhilaration — of that discovery, he forgot a crime and ignored a duty.

We look at the state of Denmark through the medium of the terrifying disclosures of the play, and few of us, I imagine, realize what a decent, God-fearing, edifying, and estimable little state the Shakespearean Denmark was in its own eyes and the eyes of its neighbors before the death of Hamlet's father. It was a pious, tedious, decorous, and punctilious court into which the younger Hamlet was born, a court at which Shakespeare himself would have been almost as bored as on that "Mayflower" voyage in which Matthew Arnold imagined his participation. Hamlet's father was a condensation of all the virtues, with a tendency to solemnity and verbiage which the passage to another life failed to chasten, and the imminence of cockcrow could not stem. The queen, the most ductile and pliable of women, rivaled her lord in the correctness of her sentiments. In this sober little world, even the villain of the piece, the king's brother, was bound to be pietist and pharisee, a man so confirmed in sanctimony that sanctimony followed him into crime. The sleepy little court committed its interests to the care of a brainless chancellor, and so lethargic was its routine that a change of monarchs by assassination could not shake the dotard from his place.

In this atmosphere Hamlet was born and reared, and the surprising thing, in view of his later rebellions and originalities, is the extent to which he imbibed and reproduced its life. The placidities and decorums of this seemingly impeccable court found in the young prince the most amiable, receptive, and tractable of pupils. His father was his pattern and ideal, and his mother was exalted among women. He was dispatched to the sedate German school at Wittenberg. His friend and mentor at Wittenberg was Horatio, a man of undoubted ability, but so judicious and wary that he may well have served rather as curb than spur to the active but submissive mind of his young comrade. As chums and playfellows he had picked out Rosencrantz and Guildenstern, two prominent members of that class which Jane Welsh Carlyle in her letters was wont to call the insipidities. Hamlet's first love affair reveals the unerring swiftness of his intuition for the obvious and the correct. His heart is granted, without reservation or parley, to the first mindless young beauty whom his eye meets in the corridors of his father's palace.

We are told in so many words that he was a model young man. He has presented the English language with two of its stereotyped phrases for the marking of a standardized perfection; he is called "the glass of fashion and the mould of form." The utterance of these words by Ophelia is as illuminative as the words themselves. It is plain that the youthful Hamlet lives up meticulously, not only to conventional, but to feminine, to maidenly, standards of propriety and excellence. He is the perfect lady's perfect gentleman.

But we do not need Ophelia's testimony; listen to the young man himself. His mother urges him not to return to college. "I shall in all my best obey you, Madam," he replies with a filial decorum which Samuel Richardson or Hannah More could not have mended. Observe the nature of his objections to suicide.

> Or that the Everlasting had not fixed
> His canon 'gainst self-slaughter.

He condemns the act, not because it is cowardly or simply immoral, but because it is uncanonical, unscriptural. Here is a young man in whom his catechist or confessor may rejoice. With such a person it is obviously hazardous to joke. When Horatio, his fellow student, calls himself a truant, Hamlet solemnly *defends him against the charge.*

> I would not hear your enemy say so.

Clearly this is a young collegian who never "vext the souls of deans." We see him assiduous at lectures, methodical in his notes. Shakespeare has not forgotten to inform us that he kept a notebook. Within two minutes after his father's ghost has ended the appalling tale of the murder in the garden, the young prince is jotting down by moonlight an invaluable memorandum about the relations of smiles to villainy. Do I mean that Hamlet is a fool? Not at all. Hamlet has a strong mind, but its strength is shown at the outset in the docility and thoroughness of its assent to the propositions of its teachers. His mind as yet is unenfranchised, unawakened, unoriginal, adverse to criticism — living happily enough in a formal and specious court which had no trouble in hiding its sins from an eye incurious — or incredulous — of evil.

This peace of mind is suddenly laid waste by crushing revelations of iniquity in his next of kin. His mother, within two months of his father's death, enters into a degrading marriage which the piety of the son brands as incestuous. His uncle has murdered his father. The first of these shocks reduces him to despair; the second plunges him into a blinding, rending anguish which expresses and relieves itself by the mimicry of distraction. At this point the first act terminates.

When the curtain rises again, we ask ourselves with a shudder to what new depth of horror and distress will this soul have sunk in the progress of its terrible adventure. What we actually see, however, is a surprise, almost a scandal, to us. The Hamlet we rediscover in the second act is actually having a good time. That good time is the paradox, is almost the unravelment and elucidation, of the play. The second act, as we perceive, is rather gay upon the whole, and is imbibed by the audience with the furtive relish with which a contraband bottle of spirits might be consumed by a drinker under a dry régime. Hamlet himself, let us hasten to add, is not happy, is not even strictly cheerful, in his good time. Mr. Shaw in his prefaces is neither happy nor strictly cheerful, yet it is certain that Mr. Shaw has an excellent time in his prefaces, and Hamlet's good time is akin to Mr. Shaw's. It is the delight of the aroused, active, and capable intelligence in the freedom, the swiftness, and, let us instantly confess, the destructive efficiency of its own action. Has he lost his mind? Hamlet has *found* his mind. The intellect which had slept or idled in the demure and decorous consciousness of a being lovely, pure, noble, and moral enough to delight an Ophelia or a Goethe has risen to self-realization, to independence, to authority. "Listen! the mighty being is awake!" The true Hamlet has come to his own. The earlier Hamlet, a mere puppet or dummy, comparable to those servants who hold places in the theater until the true occupants arrive, is swept aside into perpetual abeyance.

What relation has this fact to Hamlet's actual or simulated madness? I reject the notion of insanity, but I do not feel that its acceptance would subvert, or greatly compromise, my theory. Shakespeare undoubtedly held that the enlargement and the derangement of a mind might be simultaneous. The decisive illustration is King Lear. Lear's mind in the storm is unmistakably disordered, but who can be blind to the extension of activity, the influx of power, which make the mind of Lear for the moment the exact counterpart of the physical world which tempest has at once animated and convulsed? But, assuming the madness to be feigned, our immediate business is to show how far the theory of swift and sudden intellectual development adjusts itself to the pretense of madness.

Between his mother's second marriage and the visit of the Ghost, it is pretty clear that the young Hamlet has been solitary in the thronging fullness, and silent in the lavish intercourse, of the new court. He speaks in the first court scene only when he is spoken to, and the speeches are trains of monosyllables except where he regales his mother with a perfectly groomed little monograph on the thesis that sincerity in grief is possible. The transformation in the second act is marvelous. The recluse has become the center of the court, whom the chancellor visits and revisits, whom college friends from Wittenberg seek out, to whom a band of strolling players, seeking harborage and patronage in the palace, immediately resort, on whose moods and symptoms the king and queen in an adjoining chamber solicitously wait. Furthermore, the mute has learned the art of speech; he talks, talks with the utmost vivacity, freedom, and hardihood; leads, changes, dominates the conversation, keeps all the interlocutors in a state of amaze, subjection, and bedevilment. Assume the birth of a mind in the interval, and the mutation is logical enough. Hamlet has, in a sense, acquired new faculties, and he moves alertly and vividly in a world refreshed by the interest of these acquisitions. Clearly, in this change of conduct, a sensitive man would be glad to protect himself from the surprise of his associates. Those who had known his correct and seemly youth would think the second Hamlet crazy. Ah, there is the evident solution. The charter of insanity is large; why not avail one's self of the magnitude of that charter by feigning to have lost one's wits? The "wild and whirling words" after the Ghost's departure in the first act may well enough have been the natural product of the anguish of that unexampled night. Later on, their worth as an expedient, a subterfuge, a means of gaining the advantage of freedom of speech and action without incurring its responsibilities, would commend itself to a mind to which recklessness was attractive and caution indispensable.

The peculiarity of Hamlet's case lies in the fact that the supreme intellectual crisis, and the supreme moral and emotional crisis, of his life, being products of the same cause, have occurred at the same moment. What will be the result of this coincidence? If the subject is essentially an emotional and moral being, the crisis in the intellect will be subdued, dominated, submerged, by the crisis in the feelings and the conscience. Something of this kind occurs to Lear. But what if the core of the man's being be intellectual? What if he be primarily or finally a thinker? Surely the thinker will command, will utilize, will exploit, as we unfeelingly say, the sufferer and moralist. The emotional and moral stress, though never inactive and occasionally dominant, will on the whole be put back, be put aside, be instinctively relegated to a background from which, in moments of reaction and repentance, it will be ostentatiously drawn forth and restored to passing leadership. A scientist who is a good husband, but at bottom is less husband than scientist, finds his wife stricken with a remarkable and hitherto unstudied form of cancer. The behavior of Hamlet finds a close parallel in the probable experience of that investigator.

I have seen somewhere, in a source which I cannot now recover or identify, the suggestion that Hamlet's malady is not hesitation but preoccupation. I never read, and cannot reproduce, the grounds on which this thesis was defended. But preoccupation strikes me as a very exact description of the nature of the hindrance to activity in Hamlet's case. The difficulty lies in the *general* fertility, subtlety, and diversity of his thought, not at all in any *particular* fertility, subtlety, and diversity on the subject of the murder of the king. So far from the murder's being a simple duty which the subtlety of Hamlet's mind unduly complicates, precisely the reverse is the case. The murder is really a complex affair which the straightforwardness of Hamlet's attitude unduly simplifies. Do you tell me that he is a prey to diverse and adverse considerations on this all-important point? Will you name those considerations? You will find, I think, that they reduce themselves to two. First, Hamlet does not wish to send the king's soul to Heaven — an objection whose duration is confined to the single minute which the king spends upon his knees. Second, Hamlet wants to make sure of the Ghost's veracity by the experiment of the play, a difficulty manufactured from the start, and obsolete, by Hamlet's own confession, at the end of the play scene. On the other hand, Hamlet is quite blind to the obvious and urgent complications of the problem — the immorality of revenge (does the Everlasting forbid only *self*-slaughter?), the illegality of revenge (important surely to a future sovereign), the danger of failure, the danger of misconception of Hamlet's motive (Hamlet is heir to the crown), the danger to an invaded state from the assassination of its ruler, the mother's grief, the mother's probable exposure and disgrace. A mind to whom considerations so vital do not even occur can surely not be accused of sophistication or elaboration in its dealings with the murder. Hamlet has no will to think about the murder; he thinks of it by spasms under duress. True, the murder is always coming back to him, but a man to whom a fact must be perpetually recalled is a man with whom the fact does not willingly or naturally stay.

Hamlet, then, is not diverted from the act by thoughts about the act itself; he is distracted by other thoughts. The interests on which his mind fastens are prevailingly general or abstract. We have seen that, while he is still reeling from the concussion of the Ghost's narrative, he sets down upon his tablets a generalization about smiles and villainy. His philosophic detachment is curiously evinced in Act I, Scene 4, where he awaits the Ghost with his companions on the platform. These companions, as they awaited the Ghost in the first scene of the play, had been able to talk of nothing but the apparition; it was only after the phantom had appeared, and terror had lost the edge of novelty, that the conversation shifted to the topics of the day. But Hamlet, for whom expectation is so deeply charged, Hamlet, in a turning point of life, is asked a casual question about the reason for a cannon shot. He is instantly drawn off into a long judicial appraisement of the customs of the Danes, from which he is insensibly decoyed into a treatise on the mixture of good and evil in human nature. The agnostic Horatio must have envied the impressible and credulous Hamlet his detachment. Compare the narrative of the sea-doings in Act IV, Scene 2, with its curious parenthetic glance at the certainty of an overruling Providence.

The more the play advances, the more does the abstract reasoner, the disinterested or impersonal observer, emerge into clear view. Hamlet discusses suicide in both the first and third acts, but observe the difference. In the first act the problem is personal and concrete:

O! that *this* too too solid flesh would melt.

In Act III, the marrowless and colorless infinitive,

To be, or not to be: that is the question,

introduces a discussion of the impersonal or theoretic desirability of suicide. In the address to the players, "Speak the speech, I pray you," Hamlet has an urgent practical interest, the verification of the king's guilt. He has not talked two seconds before he has forgotten all about the king's guilt, and has lost himself in a dissertation on the art of acting. Observe his conduct in the graveyard. Hamlet, who, a few months before, had seen his father "quietly inurned," in all probability in that very graveyard, whose grief for that event is still visible in his garb, falls instantly into a train of general reflections the celerity of which not one glance, verbal or mental, at his personal bereavement is suffered to arrest.

The scene abounds in significance. On a skull, in a graveyard, Hamlet can reason about life and death, and in the process can forget a dead father. Note that the general reflections are prompted by an individual skull and graveyard, and that the encounter with these concrete starting points is casual. The mind is provoked by the eye — the straying eye; the student of laws takes his hint from fortuities. Hamlet, now restless, curious, sociable, needs or at least craves an external impetus; his mind resembles those sluggish households which spring into animation at the knock of a visitor. Even his incentives to act reach him by way of outward accident. He sees a player act Hecuba. Oh, the sensibility, the responsiveness, of men. And I —. He sees an army cross a plain to possess itself of a splinter of worthless territory. Oh, the littleness of human incentives. And I —.

The last point, though interesting, is by the way. Let us get back to the highroad. Hamlet's intelligence has been vastly quickened by the shock of two unbearable discoveries. Is there any corresponding proof of a reduction in his capacity to feel? In the court scene of the first act, which occurs between the two shocks, Hamlet's feelings are unquestionably deep. Use that emotion as a test. Do phrases like "It is not, nor it cannot come to good" or "But two months dead: nay, not so much, not two" occur in the succeeding acts? Very, very rarely. The larger part of Hamlet's utterances after Act I may be classed as impersonal criticism of life, rising often into philosophy, sinking readily into persiflage. There remains a good deal of violent and feverish declamation of which vivid examples are producible in the terminal soliloquy of Act II, the closet scene, and the close of the action in the graveyard. The case for emotion in the later Hamlet depends on the weight we assign to this declamation.

First of all, it is full of that noise and vehemence which wise men have never ranked high among the indications of sincerity. On the contrary, a distrust of the genuineness of such matter ranks fairly high among the indications of wisdom. Moreover, we have the quite extraordinary advantage of a criticism of the reality of these declamations from Hamlet himself. With a frankness hardly matchable in literature, he twice virtually confesses that his prowess in diatribe is histrionic (V, I, 271–272, Furness, "I'll rant as well as thou"; see also II, 2, 558–563). It is interesting to observe that the sonorous "I loved Ophelia" occurs just twelve lines in advance of the second of these acknowledgments. In Hamlet, while real emotion undoubtedly exists, the raiment of emotion is often donned by nervous excitability. Follow step by step in the second and third acts the accumulating efforts and excitements that mark the passage of an unexampled day, and in the vehemencies of the closet scene you will find the retaliations of the organism as distinct as the wrath and trouble of the heart.

In the later acts, Hamlet's love for Ophelia rests on the dubious evidence of a single unconfined hyperbole. His love for his father is expressed with infrequency and with temperance; the eulogy in the closet scene is strategic and forensic. What is his feeling toward his uncle? The outbursts of vilification which occur from time to time seem rather apologies for indifference than proofs of agitation. Hamlet scarcely hates his uncle. Hatred implies a certain flattery of its object which the scorn of Hamlet is reluctant to bestow. Claudius scarcely interests Hamlet. If the subject of the play be a relation between persons at all, the relation between Hamlet and Claudius is that subject. How often does Hamlet speak to his uncle? I expect the reader to break into indignant remonstrance when I assure him that, by actual count and by liberal count, Hamlet addresses Claudius only twenty-one times in the progress of the play. Ten of these twenty-one are in a short dialogue in Act IV which is never acted. On the stage, accordingly, Hamlet speaks barely eleven times to his uncle. The episodic, inattentive, contemptuous murder of Claudius—a murder which is half a slight—is one of the curiosities of literature. The stab is preceded and followed by a revelation of indifference which is itself a stab. It is interesting to ask, moreover, why the scene in which Hamlet stands with half-drawn sword behind the kneeling king, a scene which ought to be the culmination of the play, since it is the play, as usually conceived, in picturesque epitome, should move us so little in the reading, and so much less in the actual performance.

There is one fact in Hamlet's later state of mind which partly explains the blunted edge of grief and indignation. What is shocking to a philanthropist is normal for a misanthrope; Hamlet has passed from one condition to the other. A fire burns down a house. If the conflagration extends to the entire city, it is obvious that the blackened ruins of the house will stand out far less in the length and breadth of multiplied calamity than they would have done if the city had been spared. Reconstruct your world to fit an enormity, and, in a world so reconstructed, the enormity will lose much of its unexpectedness and its disgrace. The conduct of the queen and Claudius has led to a "revision downward," as people once said of the tariff, of Hamlet's early estimate of the worth of life and human nature. He condemns men in bands, in tribes, old men, young girls, courtiers; he has even a lash for humanity. Devastation has its fearful joy; the strange gayety of Hamlet is partly explicable by the exhilaration which he finds in the sack and pillage of the ideals of the race. An irruption of Montaigne into Pascal, an uprising of La Rochefoucauld in Bossuet, might have induced a kindred effervescence.

My argument is now complete; its content may be thus recapitulated:

First, the gravity, decorum, and pietism of the Danish court.

Second, the seemingly complete impregnation of the young prince with this spirit.

Third, the dormancy or latency in the young prince of a powerful mind which nothing, up to the hour of his mother's second marriage, had freed or quickened.

Fourth, the simultaneous arrival of a profound moral and emotional convulsion and of the liberation of the intellect.

Fifth, the retreat in consciousness of the moral and emotional convulsion before what was, to an essentially intellectual being, the superior interest of the enfranchised and emergent mind.

Sixth, a resultant preoccupation with the affairs of the mind which made concern with immediate duty uninteresting and laborious.

Seventh, a falling off in the distinction and significance of the crimes that had shocked Hamlet through the extension and completion of the misanthropy which those crimes had bred.

Do I believe that Shakespeare really meant what I have imputed to Hamlet in the present article? Ah, what Shakespeare meant, what one secretly and genuinely believes! I had rather argue half a day in defense of a theory than face the probe of one such deadly question. A theory is an excellent strap with which to bind facts together for convenience of transport; it is an excellent shelf on which to set them forth in compact array for summary or survey. Speculation on Hamlet is inevitable. Hamlet is a mystery; he is said to illustrate the charm of mystery: but a mystery which is put aside or left alone cannot be said to fulfill its office or exert its charm. Yet at the end of speculation comes the chastening sense of the arrogance of the attempt to explain a mind like Shakespeare's on a point on which that mind has failed or declined to explain itself.